FLYING TIME

BECOME A FLIGHT ATTENDANT

CAREER GUIDE

FLYING TIME CAREER GUIDE

First Edition
Copyright © 2019
All rights reserved.

ISBN: 978-1-9162991-8-4

Printed in the United Kingdom
10 9 8 7 6 5 4 3 2 1

Library of Congress Cataloging-in-Publication
Data
A CIP catalogue record for this book can be obtained from the
British Library

Who said it could not be done? And what great victories has he to his credit which qualify him to judge others accurately?

- Napoleon Hill

THE INSIDE SCOOP

MAKE YOURSELF UNFORGETTABLE

SURVIVAL 101

PART 4

BOOST YOUR CANDIDACY

 Application guidance

Ulterior motives - Important guidelines - Stretching the truth
Minimise a fragmented work history - Fill gaps in employment
Never admit to being fired - Age discrimination
Communicate your suitability - Use action phrases
Leverage your leisure interests - The power of a personal statement
Highlight career progression - List your awards
Get permission from your referees - Application example

 Resume guidance

Influence the direction of the interview - Appearance
A computer could be deciding your fate - Action verbs - Format
Outline - Sample resume

 Produce polished photographs

Requirements - Formal vs Informal - Set the Scene - Work the Angles
Dress the Part - Tend to your Grooming - Warm your Smile

 Power up your portfolio

Boost your experience - Get volunteer work - Learn new skills -
Enhance your education - Engage in extra-curricular activities

LIFTING THE LID ON THE GROUP INTERVIEW

What to expect

Complacency and the waiting game - Just a number
Avoid the traps during the icebreaker session
Stand out as an individual - A process of elimination

Hidden meanings behind the group tasks

What recruiters are really looking for - Where confusion often occurs
Focusing on the wrong element - Seven heavenly virtues
Seven deadly sins - Active involvement is essential...
...But don't overdo it - Your scorecard

Sample tasks

Practical Tasks - Group Discussions - Role Play Scenarios

PART 3

TAKE ON THE FINAL INTERVIEW

 What to expect   Page 279

Icebreaker or deal-breaker - Meet the recruitment team
What assessors are really looking for - Seven Heavenly Virtues
Seven Deadly Sins - Avoid robotic, flat and boring answers
Demonstrate respect for the recruiters - Eek, I don't know the answer
Run of the mill cliche's will not cut it - Stand out as an informed candidate

 Winning formula   Page 295

Answers as easy as A.B.C - A.C.T on negative questions
Winning answers with S.A.R.R formula
Probing with follow-up questions - The constant interruption

 Guidelines for the most frequent questions   Page 307

 Sample answers   Page 355

Behavioural - Traditional

 Ask the right questions   Page 389

Question Guidelines - Questions about Suitability
Questions about the Recruiter - General Questions - No Questions
Questions to Avoid

FROM THE PUBLISHER

This book is designed to provide information and guidance on attending a cabin crew assessment. It is sold with the understanding that the publisher and author are not engaged in rendering legal or other professional services. Such topics, as discussed herein are, for example, or illustrative purposes only. If expert assistance is required, the services of a competent professional should be sought where you can explore the unique aspects of your situation and can receive specific advice tailored to your circumstances.

It is not the purpose of this guide to reprint all the information that is otherwise available to candidates but instead to complement, amplify and supplement other texts. You are urged to read all the available material, learn as much as possible about the role and interview techniques and tailor the information to your individual needs.

Every effort has been made to make this guide as complete and accurate as possible. However, this guide contains information that is current only up to the printing date. Interview processes are frequently updated and are often subject to differing interpretations. Therefore, there are no absolutes and this text should be used only as a general guide and not as the ultimate source of information.

ONLINE

Updates, special offers and
newsletters will be made
available at:

www.CabinCrew.guide

So be sure to stop by.

www.CabinCrew.Guide

Where dreams are made

TO YOU

This book is dedicated to all my readers who refuse to give up on their dream.

Thank you and good luck

THE
INSIDE SCOOP
PART I

Contents

Of this Session

You can do it, if you believe
you can

- Napoleon Hill

THE
TRUTH
ABOUT THE HIRING
PROCESS

ABOUT THE ~~HIRING~~ *elimination* PROCESS

We'd all like to think that recruitment personnel are giving their undivided attention to each resume they receive, and we'd also like to think that every candidate would receive a fair and equal opportunity to interview for the position. The unfortunate truth is, each airline receives thousands of applications every month. This not only puts a great deal of pressure on recruitment teams to reduce the load, but also makes it very difficult for any one candidate to stand out.

After seeing hundreds of hopefuls, it is only natural that faces and resumes begin to blur, with each sounding and looking much the same as the next.

"The process is designed to filter and eliminate"

To address this overload, airlines have become highly selective and candidates are put through a gruelling screening process, whereby **hidden assessments** and **trick questions** provide recruitment personnel an opportunity to **secretly eliminate** large numbers of unsuspecting candidates as early as possible. In essence, the process is no longer one that is designed to screen for the right candidate or the best fit, but rather to filter and eliminate.

What was once a merely challenging process has morphed into a barrage of **trick questions, underhand tactics, psychological traps, and secret criteria.** Each designed to whittle down the numbers as quickly as possible, leaving those candidates who are unprepared and uninformed feeling bewildered and confused by the whole process.

While this process sounds unfair and brutal, it is not intended to be cruel or malicious. Rather, it has become an unavoidable means of conducting high volume and fast paced interviews within the majority of airlines. In order to understand the motives behind such recruitment processes, it helps to understand things from the airline and recruitment officer's perspective. So, let's consider the following statistics:

In 2012, Delta Air Lines received **22,000 applications for just 300 openings,** with applications arriving at a rate of 2 per minute. (Bloomberg: 2012) This is not an abnormal occurrence as Delta has also been quoted to receive **100,000 for 1,000 jobs** just 2 years earlier (ABC News, 2010). These statistics put each applicant at less than **2% chance of success.**

Meanwhile, Emirates Airline is "Swamped with cabin crew applications" (Gulf News, 2010).

"Applications arriving at a rate of 2 per minute"

Today Emirates are quoted to recieve over **15,000 applications each and every month**, with most recruitment drives attracting over 1,000 candidates. It is also recorded that, of the 400 candidates who turned up to a 2010 open day in Spain, **just 30 made it though** to the final interview. The Chief Commercial Officer of Emirates, Thierry Antinori, noted that **Emirates received over 129,000 applications** during 2013. (Trade Arabia, 2014)

Similarly, Al Baker of Qatar Airways reports "Qatar Airways was recruiting 250-300 cabin crew every month and that each open recruitment session saw around **800-2,500 candidates.** (Reuters, 2014)

As you can now appreciate, conducting recruitment drives on such a large scale is a tedious task for the personnel who oversee the process, not to mention an expensive one for the airline.

AND DECEPTIVE TACTICS

So, why donít airlines just recruit additional staff to handle the load?

All companies, not just airlines, are aware that candidates rarely show their true selves during a formal interview process. After all, it is only natural that candidates want to be seen in the best possible light. The problem is that some candidates will go so far as to put on a show in order to impress, and even mislead, the officers. These make it difficult for recruitment personnel to accurately gage whether a candidate truly is a good fit for the airline and its corporate culture, or is just playing the part for the interview.

Sadly, more recruitment personnel do not address this problem, so airlines have come up with an alternative strategy: A strategy that not only restores the power of control back to the airline, but also relieves the uncertainty.

"Airlines have come up with an alternative strategy"

The fact is, additional recruiters have already been hired, however, these additional members of the team are not part of the identifiable personnel, but are part of the **undercover team**.

To help the recruitment officers make informed decisions and better elimination choices, undercover officers are often placed among the group during recruitment days. Within the guise of a fellow candidate, these officers can observe individuals in their relaxed and natural state, and be in a better position to extract information.

Information that would never otherwise be revealed is openly volunteered by unsuspecting candidates, as they are **lulled into a false sense of security and tricked into dialogue with deadly small talk.** Any mishap can land your resume in the rejection pile and you to the nearest exit.

These officers are largely accountable for the high percentage of failure rates that candidates experience during the group stage and are the reason why many candidates leave the interview feeling confused about their elimination. More significantly, it is those **friendly manipulation and underhand tactics** that enable officers to uncover information and eliminate candidates based on **secret criteria and other discriminations**.

"Information that would never otherwise be revealed is openly volunteered by unsuspecting candidates"

AND DISCRIMINATIONS

It is no secret that airlines have stringent criteria for their cabin crew recruits. Among these, you will find minimum and maximum age, height and weight ranges, as well as health, fitness and grooming guidelines. These criteria are openly published and accessible to candidates through the airlines literature, however, **what candidates don't know, and what airlines will never reveal, are the secret criteria for which many elimination decisions are based.**

This secret criterion goes far beyond what is essential for the safe and effective conduct of the cabin crew duties, and even beyond what is considered ethical and moral. With no legal requirement to tell candidates why they were unsuccessful, most airlines have adopted a **zero feedback policy**. While this policy has been put in place due to the sheer volume of applicants, the protection this policy provides, sadly, leaves it **open to abuse.**

Every airline, from the largest international carriers to the smallest national operators, has its own **secret screening criteria**. As such, it is important to remember that, although it is illegal to discriminate, anything you share with the airline or their staff can be used against you without your knowledge. In such instances, these decisions can never be challenged or verified because such criterion are never openly discussed, nor are they written dawn. Essentially, they don't officially exist.

"Every airline has its own secret screening criteria"

Inconsistent
AND CONFUSING OUTCOMES

This lack of coherence and transparency naturally leads to very inconsistent outcomes for unsuspecting candidates, who may be viewed favourably by one officer, but not the next. Such exclusions appear to be without just cause, **leaving candidates confused and dejected** by the whole process.

"Unaware of the hidden processes that lie deep within the screeening process"

As the candidate struggles to establish a logical explanation for their dismissal, they tend to fall into a deadly cycle of overanalysing their own performance, often becoming overly self critical and then coming to the wrong conclusion entirely: A conclusion, which is often **taken out of context and to the extreme**. This leads to yet another problem, the problem of self-doubt and lack of confidence.

In the quest for answers, such candidates often seek out the comfort and guidance of others. Unfortunately, however, the guidance they receive is often from others who are just as confused as they are, as they too are unaware of the hidden processes that lie deep within the screening process. Sadly, this is also where the **myths and fear mongering** emerge, leaving the candidate feeling helpless and ready to give up on their dream.

IN THE SYSTEM

For the most part, the motives behind employing these strategies are understandable. With the high costs incurred from the recruitment drives, not to mention the expense associated with the training and licensing of new hires, It goes without saying that **any mistakes made in the hiring process work out to be a very expensive and time consuming ordeal for the airline:** An ordeal that airlines will do anything to avoid.

"Under pressure to whittle down the numbers"

The unfortunate thing is that **it is often the innocent candidates who lose out** with such a system. This is because undercover officers are under such a great deal of pressure to whittle down the numbers, that **elimination decisions can be based on minor and negligible reasons.**

For instance, most candidates will experience some form of anxiety during an interview. While such a phenomenon is entirely natural and forgivable during the early stages of the process, the outward symptoms may cause a temporary shift in the candidate's personality. While this is not a accurate representation of their true character, the candidate may be eliminated before they have chance to compose themselves.

Unfortunately, this is a process that is unlikely to change as long as demand for cabin crew positions continue to increase. So rather than be discouraged by this flawed system, **it is time to take control** so that you can **work this system to your advantage.**

WORK THE SYSTEM

TO YOUR ADVANTAGE

By understanding the process from the inside, **you can avoid being slaughtered by these underhand tactics.** You can tip the balance of power in your favour, so that you become the one who is doing the screening, not the airline. **No longer will you be cursed with generic run-of-the-mill answers and uninspiring resumes that have you looking and sounding like everyone else,** but will stand out as the top candidate that you truly are.

So whether you are a seasoned applicant who is finding yourself frustrated by another unsuccessful attempt or are a new candidate looking forward to your first interview, the **insider secrets and step by step guidance** within this book will give you a huge lead over the competition.

"No longer will you be cursed with generic answers and uninspiring resumes"

THE HIDDEN SECRETS

You will not find pages of information informing you about the duties, history and roster structures, and nor will you find average advice. **This book is raw and will take you behind the scenes to reveal secrets that airlines donít want you to know.**

The information is **universal**, revealing how candidates are screened and hired all across the world, from the largest international carriers to the smallest national operators. The information is **timeless**, so you will not find out-dated or irrelevant advice, and, most importantly, it is **uncensored**. For the first time, you be shown how to avoid the common traps and pitfalls, and the true reasons why no airline will ever tell you why you were unsuccessful in your pursuit.

The hiring process is not always correct and it is often unfair, however, if you **understand the process from the inside**, you will never have to worry about what is expected or what recruiters really want to hear, You can enter the process informed and prepared, ready to come away with the job offer.

"Prepare yourself, for you are about to understand the screening process from an entirely different perspective."

Don't worry about failures. Worry about the opportunities you miss when you don't even try

- *Jack Canfield*

THE
TRUE
ASSESSMENT CRITERIA

ASSESSMENT CRITERIA

If you visit any airline website, you will find the criteria for the position of cabin crew is openly published and available to view. The guidelines are very simple and often outline key elements, which fall into the following categories Eligibility, suitability and specific criteria.

Most candidates will find these guidelines very easy to qualify for, and most will exceed those given. So, why is the success rate for cabin crew so very low? The answer lies within the fourth criterion.

Unveilling the hidden criterion

This fourth criterion is the hidden element that airlines don't publish and don't want candidates to know. This is because the hidden criterion actually falls within the realms of discrimination. While such prejudices are considered illegal in most countries, it is unfortunate that these still do occur within most industries and organisations worldwide.

This discriminatory practice is able to continue because of the layer of protection afforded by the airlines 'no feedback' policy. Candidates can be eliminated for any reason at all, even if that reason is immoral, unethical or illegal, simply because they are never openly discussed and nor are they written dawn.

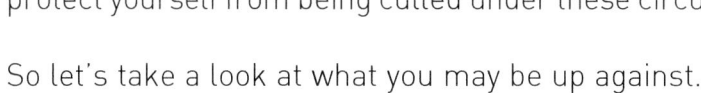

While some of these criterion are indicative of issues that cannot be overcome or changed, many of these are absolutely within your control and there are strategies that you can use to protect yourself from being culled under these circumstances.

So let's take a look at what you may be up against.

Age barriers

Due to regulations, many airlines no longer advise an upper age limit as part of their criteria; however, this does not mean that none exist. In fact, it is quite the contrary. Until recently, many airlines did advise an upper age limit, typically in the mid to late 50s, however this was rarely their preference and did not imply such candidates would be given a fair and equal opportunity.

Nowadays, airlines often imply 'young', 'youthful' and 'energetic' as part of their job description, in order to attract younger applicants, and officers are able to eliminate mature candidates at will.

Unfortunately, age discrimination does not end there. If you are a female of childbearing age, you may also face discrimination, even if you have no intention or desire to have a child. This is evidenced by the 2013 campaign by GoAir, the low cost Indian airline, which openly advertised for candidate's between 18-24 years old (WSJ, 2013).

While this level of honestly is rare, it does provide a valuable insight into what really goes on behind the scenes.

AND FAMILY LIFE

Female candidates face further scrutiny when it comes to their family life, marital status and childbearing plans. It is assumed that female crew who have family commitments are inflexible and have priorities, which run contrary to those of the position. Worse still are the assumptions made that female crew in their 30s will be likely to leave quickly due to marriage and childbearing plans.

Qatar airlines are so strict when it comes to personal relations, that they even go as far as to prohibit marriage within the first five years of employment. (Reuters, 2014)

Beware: Wearing a wedding band or engagement ring is a clear indication of your marital status, as is a picture of your child being revealed as you access your belongings.

APPEARANCE

While it is a myth that airlines only hire candidates who embody perfect figures and harbour model looks, there is no denying that airlines do favour candidates who are well groomed and portray a polished image. Candidates who arrive un-groomed or in less than desirable attire are unlikely to continue far in the process, as are those who are sporting visible tattoos or facial piercings, outrageous hair colours or styles.

For those of you who are blessed with above average appearance, it will certainly not harm your candidacy; however, do not be disillusioned that this aspect alone will provide you with an automatic admission. Such ideas will only lead you into a false sense of security and disappointment.

Another aspect of appearance that often comes up is with reference to weight. For this purpose, airlines refer to the Body Mass Index (BMI) guidelines.

The BMI is a formula used by health professionals to determine an adult's healthy body weight in relation to their height. While weight is an avenue that is certainly open to discrimination, particularly for those who fall within the higher end of the spectrum, it is unlikely to be a problem if your weight falls within the mid to lower parameters of the chart. You can determine your own proportions, by referring to the BMI chart that follows.

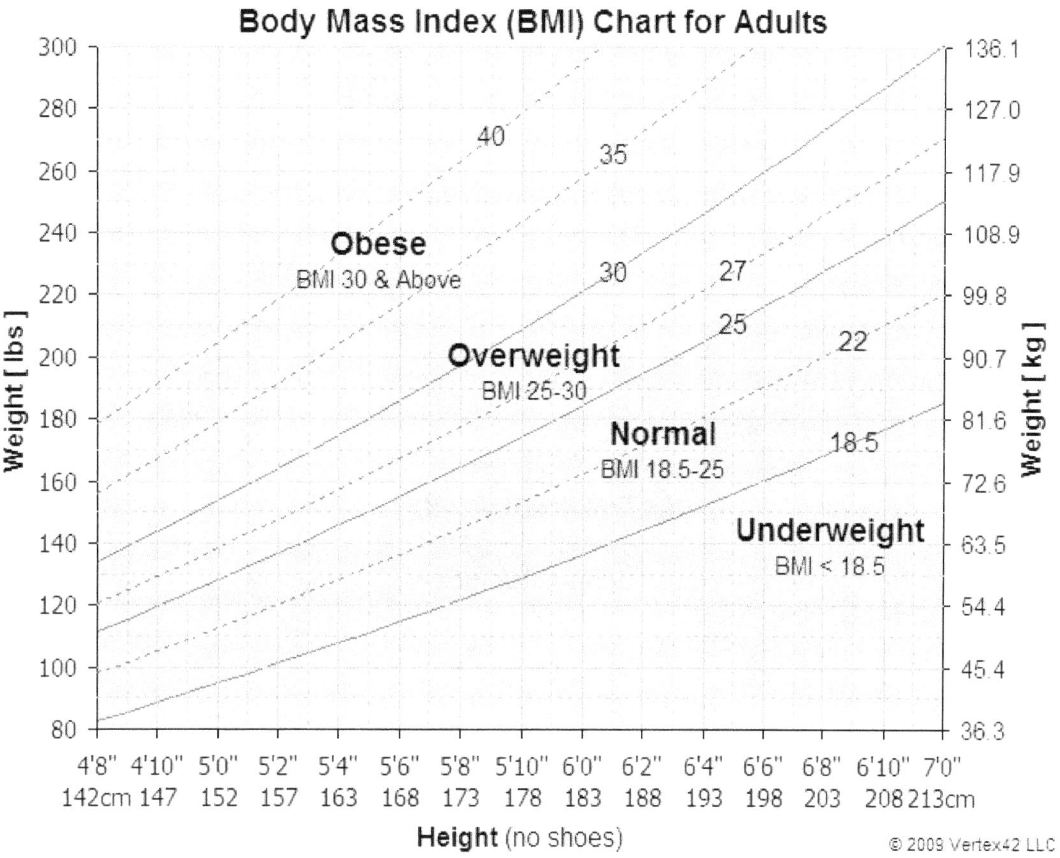

Body Mass Index (BMI) Chart for Adults

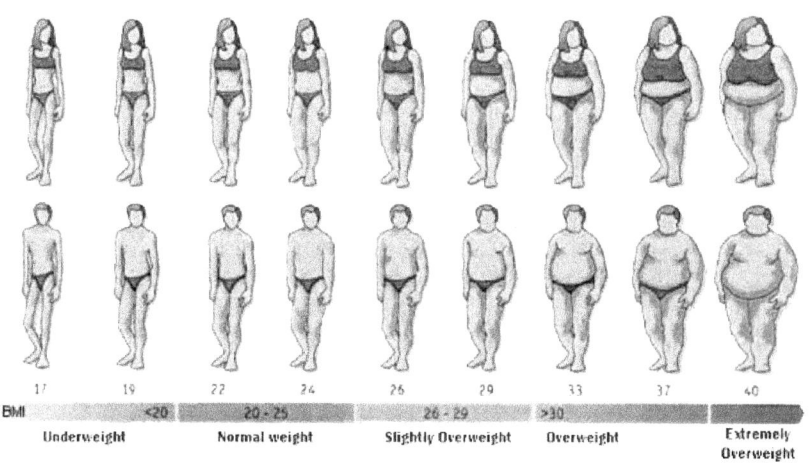

The chart plots Weight [lbs] (80 to 300) and Weight [kg] (36.3 to 136.1) against Height (no shoes).

Obese — BMI 30 & Above
Overweight — BMI 25-30
Normal — BMI 18.5-25
Underweight — BMI < 18.5

BMI lines: 40, 35, 30, 27, 25, 22, 18.5

Height: 4'8" 142cm · 4'10" 147 · 5'0" 152 · 5'2" 157 · 5'4" 163 · 5'6" 168 · 5'8" 173 · 5'10" 178 · 6'0" 183 · 6'2" 188 · 6'4" 193 · 6'6" 198 · 6'8" 203 · 6'10" 208 · 7'0" 213cm

Height (no shoes)

© 2009 Vertex42 LLC

BMI: 17 · 19 · 22 · 24 · 26 · 29 · 33 · 37 · 40

<20	20 - 25	26 - 29	>30	
Underweight	Normal weight	Slightly Overweight	Overweight	Extremely Overweight

39

Another discrimination that has been highlighted recently is that of gender. The reason for this discrimination is down to the costs associated with weight management. The rationale is that men are often heavier than their female counterparts. This was first brought to light when GoAir disclosed "significant savings of over £330,000 from hiring female only crew" (Daily Mail, 2013).

Whether this is something that we can see spreading to other airlines is uncertain, however, it is important to be aware of such exclusions if you are a male candidate.

Personal Bias

This criteria is much more difficult to define, simply because these are generally open to the interpretation and discretion of the recruitment personnel. Under this criterion, a candidate may be subjected to outright discrimination, the victim of a personality clash or for no logical reason at all.

Such biases are not defined by the airline, and often times the airline isn't even aware of their existence. They are the views harboured on a personal and individual level and not necessarily the consensus on any of the other recruitment personnel.

Unfortunately, such decisions can never be challenged or verified because they don't officially exist.

It may or may not surprise you to discover that the risk of being eliminated based on such discriminations is often within your power. Often times, a candidate is eliminated simply because of his or her own willingness to share such personal and private information. Candidates don't realise that secret eliminations and discriminations occur and nor are they aware that undercover officers are patrolling the floor extracting information from unsuspecting candidates. It is this sharing of information that inadvertently causes many candidates to be secretly and unfairly screened out from the process.

Let us take age as an example. The information represented on your resume is an easy way for recruiters to decipher your age. So, in order to conceal this, you may consider omitting dates and providing only a partial employment history. Problem solved, right? Not quite. Personnel are trained to use a variety of tactics to get you to volunteer sensitive information that would be illegal to ask in an interview. In the absence of solid information, it is the undercover recruitment personnel, trick questions and friendly manipulation that come into play.

Due to the legality of such discriminations, it is highly unlikely that you will be asked any of these questions outright. What is most likely is that the questions will come in the form of icebreakers or a friendly small talk. As such, it is important to remember that, although it is illegal to discriminate, anything you share with the airline or their staff can be used against you without your knowledge and without any evidence to dispute. So always be on guard with your sensitive information and always keep your personal life personal.

As we progress onto the upcoming sections of this book, I will go into much more detail about these undercover operations and how you can avoid falling victim to their manipulation. So continue reading...

A successful man is
one who can lay a firm
foundation with bricks
others have thrown at him

- David Brinkley

SECRET
SCREENINGS
AND BOOBY TRAPS

AND THE *red pen*

Turning up to a cabin crew interview without a pen could spell disaster for your pursuit. Not only will you look unprepared, but the apparent lack of intention to take down any notes will give the impression that you are not serious.

For this reason, the recruiters will carry a supply of red, or green, pens so that they can easily identify such candidates when it comes time for processing the eliminations. Needless to say that any forms completed in red or green ink will be immediately rejected.

To avoid this very simple blunder, it is always best to carry two pens. This will provide you with a backup should one run out of ink or become lost, or you may need to help out a fellow candidate in their time of need. Just be sure that both pens contain either blue or black ink.

SILENCE

One of the most common interview traps you will encounter is the silent treatment. With this trick, the interviewer will respond to your answer with a blank stare and a deadening silence. This trick is so incredibly effective because most candidates are so intimidated by silence that they will often rush to fill the void.

Rather than see the silence as just a pause for thought, many candidates will view the silence as an indication that they have just goofed up in some way. It is in their haste to justify and recover their answer that they then volunteer irrelevant or damaging information, often appearing flustered and knocking themselves out of contention.

The point of using silence is to see how you respond to stress, therefore, whenever you are confronted with silence, the best strategy is to remain silent yourself. If the silence persists after 5-10 seconds, you can proceed to ask "is there anything I can add to clarify this point?" or "Did I answer the question fully enough?" These questions will demonstrate that you are not intimidated by silence or stress and will put the responsibility clearly back onto the interviewer. If there is something troubling him or her, this will encourage disclosure and an appropriate opportunity for you to reiterate.

Whenever you are in the vicinity of the airline's territory, you will want to be watchful of your surroundings. Whether you are in the waiting area, at the front desk or in the restroom it is a good bet that employees, who have been enlisted to become internal spies for the recruitment team, are observing you.

The most obvious, yet often overlooked, internal spy is that of the humble receptionist. As the first and last point of contact, these powerful gatekeepers are in a prime position to observe candidates in all circumstances and from every angle. In putting on the friendly receptionist routine they are able to engage candidates in friendly dialogue, gathering information that can then be fed back to the recruitment team. Taking on a different approach, such as being rude or ignoring your presence, they will be able to entice and observe a different reaction entirely: A reaction that would otherwise not be accessible.

And what about the seemingly harmless cleaning staff in the restroom? Could they also be used for such purposes? Absolutely. In fact, It is within the so-called privacy of the restroom that candidates often vent their frustrations or bare their souls. So it is important to always be mindful of your interaction with anyone you come into contact with, even your fellow candidates. As we venture into the section entitled 'Undercover Ops', we will explore this aspect much further.

Colour-coded sticky notes

When it comes to feeding information back to the recruitment team, the receptionists use secret signals in the form of colour-coded sticky notes. If any red flags or doubts are raised about any candidate, a specific colour sticky note will be placed on their application form as a forewarning. If this happens, the candidate may be awarded a courtesy interview, but this is often as far as they will go.

Due to the nature of this trick, it is often reserved for the invitation only or final interview sessions.

INTERVIEWER ROUTINE

The friendly interviewer routine is one that catches even the most seasoned candidates off guard. You enter the interview room and are surprised to discover that you are greeted by a warm and friendly welcome. The interviewer chats openly about all sorts of things, almost as if you are just catching up with an old friend. They make you feel at ease and, as you feel like you are starting to make a connection with this friendly individual, you suddenly find yourself letting your guard down.

Maybe you feel that you've created some sort of friendship. Maybe this interviewer is looking to help you get a job. Wrong! Interviewers are trained to be enthusiastic and friendly representatives of the airline, and it is this friendly approach that lulls candidates into a false sense of security. Under these relaxed conditions the interviewer is able to get a better sense of who you really are, and before you know it you begin revealing sensitive information about your home life, financial problems, health, former employer and challenges you are facing. By the time you realise that you've said too much, it's already too late.

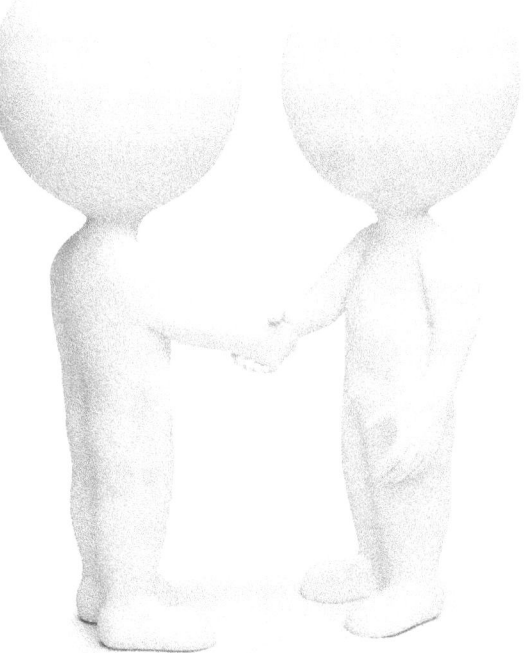

Whenever you meet the interviewer for the first time, it is important not to be taken in by this friendly approach. You certainly don't to want to appear rigid, by any means, but you do need to be mindful of who you are talking to and remain professional.

The lull of reciprocation

Following on from the friendly interviewer routine is the lull of reciprocation tactic. This tactic is probably one of the sneakiest because it is very easy to be taken in if you are unprepared. Here's how it works:

You enter the interviewer's office and the officer casually begins to open dialogue with some small talk about their children, or complains about their knee as they struggle to take their seat. Harmless? Unfortunately not! The purpose of this dialogue is to encourage a reciprocal response. For those candidates who are parents themselves, it is only natural that they too will begin to talk about your own children in response to such a comment. Or if a candidate is facing health struggles of their own, they may feel compelled to share out of empathy or politeness. 3178

These are just two examples, but there could be many more related to age, marital status, or your employment history. The list could go on.

Reciprocal remarks are quite acceptable in a social setting, but are completely inappropriate during a formal interview. So if you ever find yourself faced with this situation, the best approach is to respond with a question. For instance, in response to a comment about their children, you could ask, 1405 "How old is your son/daughter?" Likewise, in response to any statements relating to health, you could simply state "oh dear, I'm sorry to hear of your knee trouble. How did you hurt it?" These responses maintain a friendly connection, without giving anything away. In most cases, this will be sufficient to move the interview along.

MISERY LOVES COMPANY

OF A POSITIVE QUESTION

Lets say that partly through the interview when the recruiter asks how soon you can start. This is a simple question and one that has positive connotations. Unfortunately, this is an example of a trick question, which has been disguised as a positive one. When candidates hear this question, the natural response is one of excitement as they feel they are being offered the job. Without much thought, they begin to express a willingness to get started straight away.

The problem with this response is that if you are in employment your answer indicates that you are not willing to provide appropriate notice, and therefore will not be fulfilling obligations to your current employer. This surely does not work in your favour.

The best answer in response to this question is to affirm, "I have the energy and enthusiasm to start straight away. All I need is two week's notice for my current employer".

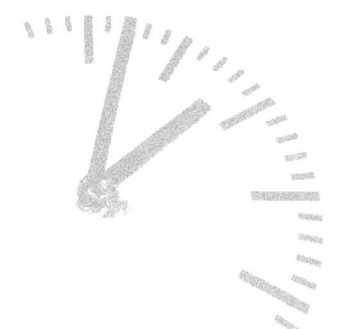

The abrupt end

The abrupt end is just how it sounds. All of the sudden, as if from out of nowhere, the interviewer declares an end to the interview. They show you to the door and thank you for your time. What should you make of this?

This sort of abrupt end is very similar to the silent treatment trick, in the sense that the interviewer is seeking your reaction to the stress of uncertainty. At this point, the formal interview really is over, however, your assessment is not. Your reaction will be observed very closely as you depart from the room and exit the premises. Do you remain composed or do you storm out of the building in defiance? Do you acknowledge the receptionist on your departure or simply ignore them?

As soon as you realise that the interview has reached its conclusion, regardless of what has happened and how you are feeling, it is important to depart gracefully for that final lasting impression.

Gather your belongings and, as you rise from your seat, straighten your clothing. Upon standing, thank the interviewer for his or her time and offer a final handshake. Make your way towards the door, stop and turn, and say your final thank you before making your exit. As you approach the front desk, acknowledge the receptionist with a sincere thank you and continue on your way. Only when you are clear of the area can you let out the scream of defiance, not before.

Does this abrupt end mean that you have been unsuccessful? Absolutely not! In fact, if handled well it could mark your success.

SCREENING TRAP

In a quest to save time and money, some airlines are now adopting telephone-screening techniques. The telephone screening allows selectors to eliminate unsuitable candidates without going to the expense of inviting them to attend an interview.

As is the case with the interview, this initial telephone screening is laden with tricks and traps. The most cunning of these traps is the time the call takes place. Recruiters will often ring at inopportune times, such as first thing in the morning, on a weekend or during teatime. The reason they do this is because they are hoping to catch the candidate in their natural, and hectic environment. Are there children screaming in the background? Do you answer the telephone in a friendly tone or an unwelcoming one? And if you are caught at a bad time, how do you handle it?

They may also use the friendly recruiter routine to encourage dialogue, the abrupt end and the awkward silence.

Each of which can be extra tricky when you cannot observe their body language or facial expression.

As you cannot predict when the call will come, you should be prepared as soon as you submit a resume or application form. At any time you get an incoming call from an unknown number, take yourself into a quiet room, and be sure to answer in a polite and friendly manner.

If you are caught at an inopportune time, politely ask the caller to hold for a brief moment while you move to a quiet location. Alternatively, if the timing is really bad, you can respectfully request an alternative date and time by saying "I do apologise, but is there a time I can reach you later? I'm very interested in the position and want to give you my undivided attention, but I'm afraid that now isn't the best time."

If you do what you've
always done, you'll get
what you've always gotten

– *Anthony Robbins*

UNDERCOVER
OPERATIONS

OPERATIONS

It is by no means a secret that candidates rarely show their true selves during a formal interview process. They will do their best to say all the right things, hide undesirable traits and say what they think the recruiters want to hear. After all, it is only natural that you'll want to be seen in the best possible light. The problem is, this makes it extremely difficult for personnel to accurately gage whether any one particular candidate is truly a good fit for the job, the airline and its corporate culture, or is just playing a very good part for the interview.

The task of filtering through hundreds or thousands of applicants is an arduous one and, to make matters worse, there are only a few short hours in which to accomplish it.

"Undercover officers pose the greatest threat to your success"

To relieve some of this pressure, undercover personnel are often placed among the group during recruitment days. It is these undercover officers who pose the greatest threat to your ultimate success, as their primary objective is to filter and eliminate candidates as quickly as possible, and for any reason they see fit. They are largely accountable for the high percentage of failure rates and are the reason why many candidates leave the interview feeling confused about their elimination.

ASSESSMENTS

From the moment you step foot on the airline's territory, these officers are watching and judging your every move.

Your personal conduct, how you interact socially and professionally, and the information you reveal. are constantly being scrutinised and assessed. Any mishap or red flags raised during this crucial encounter can land your resume in the rejection pile and you to the nearest exit. There are no second chances.

Within the guise of a fellow candidate, these officers can observe individuals in their relaxed and natural state, and be in a better position to extract information. Unsuspecting candidates openly volunteer information that would never otherwise be revealed, as they are lulled into a false sense of security with seemingly harmless dialogue only to be enticed into mindless gossip and other undesirable behaviours.

During this critical period, officers are observing the reactions of candidates closely as they are encouraged to reciprocate and reveal all sorts of personal and private information. The observations made are then periodically fed back to the recruitment team, who are able to use the information to make informed decisions and better elimination choices in record speed.

WHAT YOU THINK

These officers are not interested in your level of education, previous successes, or best attributes; they are there to uncover information that could potentially cause problems or inconvenience for the airline. As such, the information gathered at this level is not necessarily sized up against the airline's corporate culture and assessment criteria, but rather the hidden criterion and person specification.

It is the information candidates reveal about their health, age, their likes and dislikes, and sensitive information about their background and personal life that are of interest to these officers. Likewise, they will be very interested to learn how you react to certain kinds of behaviours, people and pressures.

Needless to say, a candidate who displays undesirable behaviour or reveal questionable information will not proceed very far.

Shocking

REVELATIONS

It never seizes to amaze me how much information unsuspecting candidates will reveal when they think they are not being assessed. In many instances, it isn't even necessary to cajole candidates into confessing information, as many will openly share all sorts of things. Is it really any wonder airlines use undercover personnel?

Here are just some of the revelations I have encountered during my on site excursions.

 ### Under the influence

"I'm so nervous I think I must have drunk a whole bottle of wine before I arrived."

 ### Bunking off work

"I had to take a sickie at work just to attend this interview, so it better be worth it."

 ### Admissions of deceit

"I had to lie on my application just to get invited to this interview"

Malicious Backbiting

"Did you see what that girl is wearing? What was she thinking?"
"That girl obviously has no brains. I bet she can't even read."

Negative intentions

"This is such a joke, I wanted to work for . . . but keep failing the damn interview so I have no choice but to apply for this one."
"I just want to work my way into first class so I can meet a rich, good looking guy"

The hangover

"I'm so hung over from last nights bash, I just want to go to sleep. Wake me when it's over."

Slandering the boss

"My stupid boss fired me, so I need this job desperately"

Many of these cases are rather extreme, I admit, however, they are by no means rare - I'm sure you've heard similar comments yourself.

As anyone can appreciate, it is these very mindless and irresponsible comments that undercover officers are seeking.

CASUALTIES

Unfortunately, candidates don't need to be malicious or brash to be excluded from the process. A candidate who innocently mentions their looming personal challenges, such as going through a separation, in a custody battle, recently been made redundant, experiencing financial difficulties, or dealing with a close family member who is in poor health, could raise red flags as to their focus and stability. While such challenges are common and entirely understandable, such circumstances are simply deemed too risky for an airline.

While the above shock statements were made by actual caniddates, is it possible that such revelations could also be made by the undercover officers themselves as part of their mini assessment? Absolutely. It is precisely this kind of revelation that officers will use to entice a reaction or a reciprocal response. Be mindful, however, because such assessments aren't always this obvious or extreme. Assessments can be covert and very sneaky, so you always need to be on your guard.

Just as new cabin crew hires are put through an intensive training program, so too are undercover officers. These officers are trained in behavioural analysis and psychological profiling and, with this training, they are able to take on a variety of different roles and employ many different tactics. This makes them very effective at blending in and there is little chance that you will ever be able to identify them with any certainty.

The good news is that simply being aware of their presence and being prepared with a strategy will give you an advantage like no other. In fact, your informed knowledge and inability to be culled by their tricks and traps will make you stand out as a top candidate among the crowd.

Even better still, there is much more that you can do, not only to evade their traps, but also turn them into your greatest ally. All that is required is a conscientious and diligent approach.

Your greatest ally

While it is accurate to say that the purpose of these undercover officers is to expose unsuitable candidates, they also have the power to approve candidates they deem to be exceptional.

If you are able to evade the tricks and traps laid out during this critical process and maintain a friendly, confident, and positive dialogue there will be no reason to pursue you further with trick questions. They will simply move on to another candidate when they are able to remove themselves from your presence. And if you are able to go one step further and create a connection with the officer, not only will you be put forward as a recommendation, but they will actually try to help you to succeed.

So how do you go about impressing these officers?

THE RIGHT IMPRESSION

To impress undercover officers, you simply need to treat everyone you meet in the same positive manner. If you are friendly, respectful and supportive towards your fellow candidates, have a positive outlook and are able to demonstrate an enthusiastic attitude towards any activities that you are asked to undertake, the officers will naturally pick up on your positive energy.

Moreover, it is important to remember that anything you say, even in jest or small talk, can and will be used against you. Thus you should avoid volunteering inappropriate information, and your personal life should remain personal.

Naturally this can be easier said than done, so I have devised a line-up of potential scenarios to help you recognise and diffuse any situation you may encounter.

Excellent

Very good

Good

Average

Poor

Undercover officers are like actors. They come in many shapes and sizes and their pseudo personalities are just as diverse. Because you'll never really know whether a candidate is truly a candidate or an undercover officer, it is important that you treat everyone the same. Here is the line-up of the common personalities that you may come across and how to deal with each of them in an appropriate manner.

The Show-Off

You can be certain to find a show-off at every cabin crew interview. You will recognise him or her by their showy, self-absorbed and obnoxious attitude. While this personality type is easily annoying, the truth is that these individuals tend to be deeply insecure. They brag about their own achievements through fear that nobody will otherwise notice. Be kind and sincerely acknowledge their efforts when appropriate. This will demonstrate that you are not easily antagonised, but are also sensitive to the feelings of others.

The Rival

In playing the part of the rival, the officer will demonstrate a very competitive streak, which puts you and everyone else as their competition and a threat to their success. They will attempt to make you feel inferior in order to throw you of guard. With these personality types, it is important to be friendly, but respectful of their space. Remember, competitive people are passionate, driven and innovative, so embrace these positive traits and don't let their feeling of superiority run you down.

The Show-Off

Gossipmongers like to point out other people's flaws or failures in an attempt to feel superior. This personality type is a favourite amongst officers because it can reveal a great deal about a candidate. Are you passive or assertive? Do you engage in gossip or show disapproval?

The best defence in this scenario is to first neutralise the negative comment by pointing out a positive and contrary opinion and then attempting to change the subject. If you have a tenacious officer, they may continue to press. In this instance, it would be wise to respectfully state that you would rather not discuss the merits of others, as it is not your place to do so. This honest approach should dissolve any further discussion on the subject. Failing that, it would be best to take your leave immediately.

The Think-They-Know-It-All

Know-it-all's have an attitude of superiority and like to think they are experts in everything. In conversation, they are arrogant and condescending and openly disregard the opinion of others. Remain cordial and patient and, whatever you do, don't be drawn into a debate, become critical or impatient. If the so called expert becomes overbearing or it is obvious that they are not an expert at all, you assertiveness skill s may be being tested, so you may tactfully and respectfully state the facts as you perceive them.

The Overly Anxious

The part of an anxious candidate is a prime opportunity to observe your patience and sensitivity. Experiencing a heightened level of anxiety is very traumatic and paralysing, so be friendly and supportive with these individuals. Offer words of encouragement, but don't place too much focus on their anxiety. Rather, try to break their state by asking questions about things they enjoy and that make them feel relaxed. You could ask them about their hobbies or desires.

The Negativist

Ah, the negativist. There's always one in every crowd and officers love to use this one to gauge a candidate's ability to remain positive under pressure. At best, negativists are very annoying. At worst, they will drain every ounce of energy and motivation from your body. If your attempts to motivate or encourage these people fall flat, remain positive and try to distance yourself as much as possible. If this is not possible, detach yourself from their words and stay focused on your own positive energy.

The Aggressor

Passive aggressors are covert and manipulative. They disguise their attacks as constructive criticism or harmless jokes so that, in the instance that they are confronted, they can deny any wrong doing. If you find yourself under attack from these predators, you may ask questions that will temp them into the open, such as: "Forgive me, but that sounded like a disrespectful comment, was it?" In the worst case, you may try to distance yourself.

If the aggressor is more openly disrespectful and disparaging, the best approach is to remain calm and composed, listen attentively and without interruption until they have finished. A counter attack will only reflect badly on you, so resist the tendency to fight back. Instead, acknowledge their opinion and then voice your own in a respectful manner or simply remove yourself from them as much as possible.

The Open Book

If an individual airs all their dirty laundry to you, revealing all sorts of personal hardships, it could be that they are looking for a reciprocal response. You may demonstrate empathy for their situation, but avoid getting drawn too deeply into conversation about of their hardship and avoid revealing any of your own. Changing the subject and pointing out the positive is always the best course of action.

The aforementioned scenarios are rather obvious, so they are generally easier to contend with. Where the traps really lie are in those personalities, which are not negative at all. In fact, it is the positive personalities, such as those in the following scenarios, which will often catch a candidate off guard. Because these personality types are friendly, approachable and easy to get on with, it is very easy to lose yourself in conversation with such individuals. It is with these personality types that you really need to be on your guard. So lets take a look at the contenders.

The Extrovert

Extroverts are very sociable creatures and thrive on interaction. They are comfortable speaking to large audiences, are very open with their thoughts and feelings, and take an enthusiastic approach to most activities. This personality type is easy to get caught up in dialogue with, so you need to be extra cautious about the information you openly reveal when in their intoxicating presence. Enjoy the buzz they create and allow their enthusiasm to radiate through you and if you have an introverted tendency, just bide you time and make an effort to enjoy their vibrant presence.

The Entertainer

Just like extroverts, entertainers are sociable, talkative and very energetic people. They love to be the centre of attention and often have an infectious personality. It is very easy to like the entertainer as they have a very down to earth and friendly attitude. When interacting with an entertainer, avoid being overly serious and just allow their positive energy to flow through you. An officer will use this type of personality to lure you into a false sense of security, so beware.

The Model

In using the term 'model', I am not referring to looks. Rather, I am referring to those candidates who seem to be models of perfection. They appear to say and do all the right things, seemingly without a care or worry in the world. They naturally exude charisma and confidence, and have a magnetic personality. Officers will use this personality type for two reasons. The first is so officers can gauge other candidates reactions to their presence, and two, they will be providing an example for others to learn from. In observing these candidates, examine what makes them appear perfect and be appreciative of those traits.

The Leader

Natural leaders are instantly recognisable by their innate desire to step up. Their confident, assertive and intelligent character inspires trust in others, while their sensitive, inspiring and sincere side inspires confidence. Officers will often use this approach to test a candidate's ability and willingness to support and encourage their fellow candidates without viewing them as competition. In the presence of a good leader, respect, support and encourage their efforts. Participate and be an active member of their team and you may just join them in the next round.

These are just some of the personality types that you may come across, but there may be many more. So always be on your guard with everyone you come in contact with.

QUESTIONS & DIALOGUE

Handling a personality type is one thing, but answering their intrusive questions or resisting deadly dialogue is quite another. So here are a few tips that will help you in this most critical part of the process.

Q: So, what do you do for a living?

This question is so common and seemingly innocent that it is easy to get caught out with. If you are between jobs, dislike your current job, or are desperate to find a new job this question can lead to and encourage negative dialogue. When answering this question, just remember to keep the discussion positive and be careful not to reveal too much about your personal circumstances if they are less than ideal.

Q: Don't you just hate interviews?

Let's be honest, unless you are like me and attend them for fun or research purposes, it is unlikely that you will relish attending interviews. However, just as you would attempt to diffuse a negative interview question with a positive response, you should do the same here. So, rather than admit to disliking interviews, you can state that you simply see it as a necessary part of the process in achieving the job that you desire and, therefore, you appreciate its necessity.

Q: This is my seventh attempt. How many interviews have you attended?

If an applicant asks you any questions regarding your previous interview attempts or current interview strategies you really must not divulge such information. You could attempt to change the subject in the first instance or, failing that, you may be polite and state that you would rather not focus on the past as you are trying to remain focused on the present.

Q: I had to take a sickie to attend this damn thing, how did you manage to take time off?

This question has many motives and your best response is a neutral one. Simply state that you have been preparing for this day for some time and have allocated time into your schedule for its purpose. There is no need to say any more.

Q: I want this job because ... What about you?

An honest and passionate response to this question will surely set you apart, so by all means share this passion if you feel it is appropriate to do so. Clearly the lure of travel is not appropriate, but you may be surprised that some individuals still use this line.

Q: My daughter decided to misbehave, today of all days. Do you have children?

This question is trying to elicit further information about your personal life. Rather than divulge this personal information you may choose to ignore it and just empathise by saying " Kids sure do pick their moments don't they? But you've got to love them". You may then attempt to change the subject. Asking follow-up questions will only encourage further dialogue and you will want to avoid this where possible.

Q: Why do we have to sing and dance? Surely this isn't part of our job description

This comment is trying to entice you to speak negatively about a task. This doesn't necessarily have to be about singing and dancing, it could be about any task. Even if you share their viewpoint, remain positive by indicating that you find such challenges fun and are eager to get involved. Nobody will know how you really feel if you don't share it.

If you encounter a tenacious officer who continues to press your buttons or if you feel backed into a corner at any time, there may be no alternative but to relieve yourself from their presence as soon as possible.

In planning your escape, you will want to make it as seamless and natural as possible so that you can avoid, or at least minimise, causing offence. You could do this during a task or a session break when the individual is conversing with other candidates. This will make it less likely that your disappearance will be noticed. Whatever you do, be sure to have a plan in mind or you risk being left alone and looking like a lost puppy: This surely won't do you any favours.

Sure there will be a risk that a real candidate may feel insulted or upset if they catch on to your disappearing act, however, if your escape is truly justified, then such candidates are not worthy of your concern as they will only bring you down. On the other hand, an officer will at least recognise your ability to distance yourself from negative situations.

Now that you understand what you are up against, it is time to learn how to make yourself unforgettable...

MAKE YOURSELF

UNFORGETTABLE

PART 2

Of this Session

Polish your appearance

Create the right impression

Create a memorable impression

A strong, positive self image is the best possible preparation for success

- Joyce Brothers

POLISH YOUR
APPEARANCE

THE MYTHS

Before we continue on I feel it is important to address some of the myths that are circulating with regards to appearance.

These myths usually imply that airlines only hire crew who embody perfect figures and harbour model looks. This is, quite frankly, utter nonsense. While there is no denying that airlines require candidates to be well groomed and portray a polished image, this element is usually taken out of context and to the extreme.

For candidates who have been victims of the hidden criteria, and already harbour self-doubts about their appearance, this myth often remains one of the few logical explanations that they can establish. This is often exaggerated further if other attractive candidates are seen to be successful.

Unfortunately, such misconceptions are highly destructive, not only to the candidates who may feel inadequate or self-conscious about their own appearance, but also for those who are blessed with above average appearance. Such candidates are unfairly alienated by candidates who feel intimidated in their presence or, worse still, feel themselves superior, thereby leading them into a false sense of security.

Whatever your appearance concerns, the good news is that there are many simple things you can do to dramatically enhance your outward appearance, and you don't have to resort to surgical intervention.

Okay, now that those myths have been officially debunked, we can press on.

FIRST IMPRESSION

During the first few minutes of meeting you, the recruitment team will make judgements about your character and suitability based on your overall presentation and appearance. This means that your standard of dress, level of grooming and how you portray yourself through your body language and carriage are all being scrutinised. Therefore, if you are to succeed in creating that all-important positive first impression, it is essential that you make an extra effort to establish a presence.

There is no doubt that appearing professional is the key to creating the best impression at a cabin crew interview. The trouble is, being professional is only part of it. Put a robot into a suit and it too would look professional, but would the robot get the job? It is unlikely.

The fact is, airlines are not looking to hire a suit, but rather they are looking to hire an individual with a personality and character. So why do so many candidates arrive at the interview dressed in the same boring attire? Because it is safe and many are afraid to change the status quo.

Think about it for a moment. How many times have you attended an interview only to be faced with countless other black suits and white shirts? Too many to count I'll bet. Suddenly, that feeling of confidence you had when you set out soon vanishes, leaving you feeling like just another face in the sea of people. If you think it's bad from your point of view, just take a look from the recruiter's perspective.

Establishing a presence is much simpler than many realise, but few ever successfully achieve. Why do so few succeed in this vital area? Because of misunderstandings and misinterpretations.

AND MISINTERPRETATIONS

The only true common denominator for interview attire is the word 'professional'. But what does it actually mean to look professional? Does looking professional indicate that you must wear black or 50 shades of grey? It most certainly does not. Does it mean that you have to dress like clerical admin staff? Heck no. So why do 95% of individuals do just that? Because that is the advice commonly given out by mainstream career advisors.

The trouble with mainstream advice is that it assumes a one-size-fits-all approach, and one size certainly does not fit all. Mainstream advice would have you believe that wearing designer garments or appearing fashionable is too much, that wearing red lipstick is too sexual and wearing any other colour beyond the achromatic range will result in rejection. They even suggest that females de-sexualise themselves in order to appear more professional and authoritative. If you are interviewing for an administrative or managerial post, this 50 shades of grey and the no makeup look may work well, but this is a cabin crew interview and this age old, run-of-the-mill advice simply does not cut it.

Rather than continue to follow this out-dated advice, it is time to make changes. Changes that will no longer leave you looking like everyone else, becoming just another face in the sea of people. Instead, you will establish a presence that gets you noticed for all the right reasons.

It's time to stand out, by not fitting in.

BY NOT FITTING IN

Dressing in a certain way solely because that is what you think is expected of you Is not the way to stand out. In fact, wearing something that is not conducive to your personality and style will not only make you feel uncomfortable, it will also strip you of your personality. Professional or not, if you are not feeling at your best it will show and you will not be maximising your opportunity.

Now I am not suggesting that you wear a bold red dress or a bright blue suit, and neither am I suggesting that you throw away your black power outfit. What I am suggesting is that you maximise your outfit according to your personal style and confidence level.

If wearing a black suit or achromatic mix makes you feel supremely confident and powerful then that is perfectly fine, but if you are only wearing this type of outfit for the sake of keeping up appearances, it is unlikely that you will feel comfortable and unable to function at your best.

Ultimately the best outfit to wear is the one that you feel the most comfortable and confident in. Clearly there are some limits and guidelines that need to be observed, however, if you feel at your best in what you are wearing, your aura will shine through and that is what will make you memorable.

Now before you dash off to the nearest shopping mall to purchase that fab outfit that I know you've had your eye on, take heed and consider the following important guidelines.

LADIES

▨ Consider: Style

Presence is achieved when you look and feel good, so it is important to wear an outfit that you feel the most confident and powerful in. However, in order to stand out for the right reasons, it is important to achieve balance: Balance between how the outfit makes you feel and what impression it creates.

Your outfit should be thoughtful and demonstrate that you have made an effort. So buy the best quality garnets that you can afford, and be sure they are clean and neatly pressed. The idea is to look business-like, yet stylish.

Tasteful, elegant and sophisticated are good objectives to aim for, and you'll want to avoid appearing flashy or overly sexy. Well-coordinated and tailored separates achieve this perfectly, as does a fitted dress in a conservative style: Conservative implying a modest neckline and appropriate length. A quality tailored jacket is a powerful piece that can tie a look together and create a streamlined and professional appearance.

Avoid heavy patterns, as these can appear overwhelming, and be sure to select wrinkle resistant fabrics, such as wool. Nothing looks more unprofessional or unprepared than rumpled clothes or wrinkled shirts.

Consider: Colour

Colour is a powerful tool that can dramatically increase your chances of standing out. Used appropriately, colour will help you to convey confidence, express your personality and enhance your complexion. So, consider adding a splash of your favourite colour to your outfit for added pizazz.

How much colour you wear will depend on you. There is not necessarily anything wrong with wearing a red pencil dress provided you have the strength of character to pull it off and the colour is flattering against your complexion. However, such a bold statement piece should not be underestimated and must be worn with caution. If you choose to wear a bold piece, be sure that you have the courage of your convictions because you will certainly be noticed and expectations will be set much higher. You wouldn't want to be noticed for looking extremely uncomfortable or for looking washed out by an unflattering colour.

You don't need to be draped in colour to make an impact. In fact, the safest way to wear colour is to add subtle splashes through your accessories, accents or pop pieces. Subtle accents can bring out the sparkle in your eyes and liven up your outfit, without appearing overwhelming or degrading your professionalism.

Whatever you ultimately decide, a contrasting style will bring a sense of balance to the outfit. For a bold and striking colour, opt for a very conservative cut and for a pale tint, add life by selecting a striking style..

Consider: Shoes

The benefits of wearing heels are obvious. They make your legs look longer, shapelier and more feminine, so it is a good idea to wear them if you feel comfortable to do so. Killer heels may have the added butt lifting effect, however, this is not the look you want to achieve at an interview. Heels should be no higher than 3" and thin soles will appear more professional and elegant than thick platforms.

For those of you who are not used to wearing heels or are on the taller side, 1" inch heels will still provide the benefits of wearing heels without the excess height.

Only wear shoes which are clean and in good condition. Tatty shoes, with scuffed toes or heels will detract from the polished image you are trying to create. Open toes, sling backs and splashes of colour are perfectly acceptable as long as they are tasteful and not overly sexy or decorative fashion styles.

Consider: Hosiery

If wearing a dress or a skirt, pantyhose in plain nude or black are essential for creating a polished and professional image, as they will ensure your legs look perfectly smooth and blemish free. Be sure to select a good quality pair, as they will hug your curves better than cheaper alternatives and will be less likely to create the unsightly wrinkled effect around the knees and ankles. Be sure to spot check them before the interview to ensure that there are no runs or ladders and always have an emergency pair in your handbag for good measure.

Consider: Accessories

Jewellery is a great way to spice up a boring black ensemble, giving it character and pizazz, however, be sure to keep your pieces minimal and conservative. Wear no more than one ring per hand, and one set of earrings, and avoid oversized fashion pieces. Bangles that clink can become distracting and annoying, so it is best to avoid them. A timepiece can be worn, but be sure the style is appropriate and turn off any audible sounds.

Observe caution when wearing an engagement ring or wedding band, as such pieces will draw attention to your private life and will leave you open to discrimination.

Consider: Grooming

Grooming is an essential aspect when presenting a polished image. They are the finishing touches that tie your appearance together. Bitten nails, unsightly blemishes and scruffy hair can undermine even the very best of outfits. So be sure to pay extra special attention to the following areas:

Nails should be clean, neatly trimmed and reasonable in length. Nail polish should match in colour and it is best to avoid charms, glitter and multi-coloured polish.

Use cosmetics to conceal blemishes and enhance your assets, but avoid going over the top. Tastefully applied makeup is the best way to achieve a polished and sophisticated look. A touch of mascara and some eyeliner paired with a dash of lipstick is all that is needed. Remember, you are attending an interview not going out for a night on the town. Refined elegance will work better than dramatic.

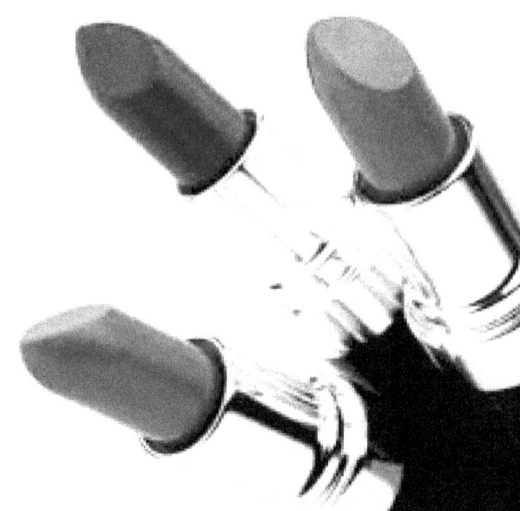

Tip: Red lipstick is a favourite among most airlines so wearing it to the interview is a fantastic psychological finishing touch. Be sure to visit a cosmetics counter to find the ideal shade of red for your complexion. The wrong shade will be noticeable as it will wash you out and ruin the effect.

Hair should be neat and well groomed, and outrageous colours or styles should be avoided. Frizzy or loose ends can appear messy so brush and fix them into place if necessary. Freshly trimmed hair will be easier to style and keep looking fresh, so book into the salon if necessary.

If you choose to wear perfume, select a light scent and wear it sparingly. There is nothing more off-putting than an overpowering odour, even a pleasant one.

Visible tattoos and facial piercings are not acceptable. Tattoos will need to be concealed and piercings removed. That applies to multiple earrings too.

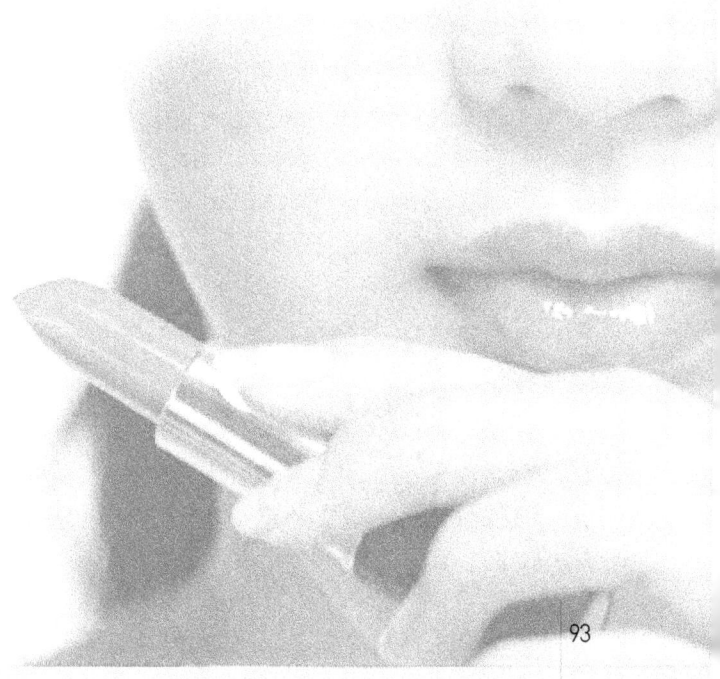

Consider: The ultimate advantage

Interviewers need to be able to visualise you in the position, so the very act of looking like you are already cabin crew will create a great psychological advantage.

Now, I am not implying that you find a suit in a matching colour to the airlines' uniform with hat and scarf to match. Sure this would make you stand out, but not for the right reasons. Subtlety is the key to success with this strategy. You're trying to capture the airlines aesthetic appeal, not look like you are attending a fancy dress parade.

The best way to pull this off is to look at the cabin crew who already work for the airline. Is red lipstick a part of the uniform? What are the typical hair grooming styles? Are their corporate colours muted, pale or bold? And what about the corporate culture? Is the airline energetic, carefree and fun loving, or conservative and professional? Understanding these aspects will help you to achieve the most appropriate interview look for each airline.

Injecting a splash of the corporate colour into your accessories is a great touch. Another is to tend to your grooming in the same way you would if offered the position. Understanding the corporate culture will further enable you to tailor your outfit according to the tastes of the airline. If the airline is famous for its fun and carefree corporate culture, you can be sure they will be more accepting of bold colours and unique styling, whereas an airline known for its conservative image may not be.

The effort you put in to this will show and it will be apparent that you have done your research to understand the airline's culture. The psychological impact this one trick can achieve is astonishing and should not be underestimated.

Avoid: Fashion faux pas

If you would like to be taken seriously, you need to avoid the following fatal mistakes.

1. Push up bra and plunging necklines

2. Bare midriff

3. Too much makeup or hair product

4. Unnecessary accessories

5. Wrinkled or unkempt clothes

6. Ill fitting garments

7. Cheap and translucent blouses

8. Scuffed or tatty shoes

9. Short skirt

10. Extremely high heels or large platforms

11. Bitten or over the top nails

12. Strong perfume

GENTS

When it comes to looking professional, the options for gents are no doubt limited. Formal business attire is essential for creating a professional, polished and streamlined look, however, when every other male candidate is also wearing business attire, how do you stand out from the crowd? It is the attention you pay to the finer details that will show that you have made an effort, and it is this that will get you noticed.

Consider: Fit & Quality

The key to looking your best in a suit is to pay special attention to fit and quality. A well-tailored suit, in a wrinkle free fabric, will create a polished and professional look that will surely set you apart from the rest. Off the rack suits are a popular choice because they are convenient and inexpensive, however, a ready to wear suit is often the worst option when making a good impression is your top priority. As such, it is advisable to purchase the best quality suit you can afford. A custom tailored suit is the obvious choice, however if finances will not stretch to this, purchase an off the rack suit and have some tailored alterations carried out for an inexpensive alternative.

Whichever option you choose, be sure to pay attention to selecting a good quality fabric. Natural fabrics are far better than synthetic fabrics or blends. In particular, wool, such as merino, cashmere and angora, will offer the best in comfort, wrinkle resistance, and longevity.

Consider: Shirt

A good quality, 100% cotton shirt, with long sleeves is essential for appearing professional and crisp. White, ecru and blue are classic and conservative choices and should be your first choice.

Dark shirts are somewhat taboo as they are often considered a style choice, rather than a professional one. As such, you need to proceed with caution if this is what you feel most comfortable wearing. On the one hand it is important to wear what you feel confident and powerful in, but on the other, it is important to achieve balance: Balance between how the outfit makes you feel and what impression it creates. Airlines are no doubt much more open to personal style choices, however, it is a choice that may not be viewed favourably, no matter how powerful and confident it makes you feel. Therefore, it is far better to play it safe.

When it comes to choosing a collar, remember that it will frame your face. As such, you will want to select a collar that brings balance to your face shape. A wide spread collar will compliment a thin and long face well, while a classic point works better on a round face.

Consider: Pattern & Colour

With regards to colour and pattern, it is best to err on the side of caution. Traditional colours, such as navy blue or charcoal grey, are great alternatives to the standard black, while brown, beige and taupe will appear too casual. If you do decide to wear black, try opting for a subtle pinstripe pattern to break up the monotony and strength of the colour.

 ## Consider: Tie

The tie is an extremely important accessory, as it is often the first thing that a person notices.

Since it frames your face, it is important to consider the colour choice carefully because the wrong colour can suck the sparkle out of your complexion, leaving you looking dull and lifeless. When considering colour, assess how it interacts and enhances your complexion. Does red make your skin look bright, vibrant and well rested? or does it make you look sallow and washed out? Likewise, does blue bring a sparkle to your eyes, or does it make your complexion look muddy and ashen?

Pattern is another factor that needs consideration. Character ties and exotic patterns, while demonstrating personality, are not the ideal interview choice. Instead, opt for subtle stripes, simple designs or block colours for a classic and professional look.

For a strong and confident appeal opt for a larger knot, such as the Pratt or Windsor and aim for a length that falls to the same level as the belt buckle. Tie bars and clips may also be worn to keep the tie in place.

Consider: Shoes & Socks

Shoes should be worn in a style and colour that coordinates with the overall look of your suit. Lace up shoes are the classic and safe option, however, loafers can also be worn if they are suitable. A thin sole will create a more professional image than thick rubber soles.

Nicked heels and scruffy toes will ruin the whole outfit, so invest in a new pair if necessary and never underestimate the importance of a good shoeshine.

Socks should be inconspicuous so they don't draw any attention. As such, they should be dark in colour and long enough to cover your calves so that your flesh is not exposed when seated.

Consider: Accessories

Accessories are finishing touches and should be treated as such. This means that they should remain simple to complement your outfit. Cufflinks may be worn if you are wearing a buttonless shirt, and a leather belt with an understated buckle ought not be forgotten.

While a leather briefcase is unnecessary, a leather portfolio will look much more professional than carrying lots of loose papers.

When it comes to jewellery, the simpler and less of it, the better. One ring and a tasteful wristwatch is all that is necessary to project a professional image.

Consider: Grooming

When it comes to grooming a good haircut and clean-shaven face are essential. A few days prior to the interview, have your hair freshly cut or trimmed and be sure to shave on the morning of the interview. Be careful not to cut yourself and try to prevent razor burn.

Nails are another aspect that is often neglected and underestimated by male candidates. A manicure is an attention to detail that will be noticed and appreciated, so visit a manicurist a few days before the interview.

If you must wear cologne, be sure not to use too much as it can be distracting and suffocating.

Consider: The Ultimate Advantage

Interviewers need to be able to visualise you in the position, so the very act of looking like you are already cabin crew will create a great psychological advantage. Now, I am not implying that you arrive in something too similar to the airlines' uniform; however, it doesn't hurt to capture an element of the industries aesthetic appeal. The one item that captures this look the best is a fitted waistcoat. It is an element often under-utilised, but its stylish appeal works wonders within the airline industry.

Some of you may baulk at this idea, however, it is an element, which will get you noticed. Not only do they create a business-like and streamlined appearance, but it will show that you have made an extra special effort. Take a look at the Virgin Atlantic uniform to get a sense of its style for yourself. If a waistcoat does fit in with your personal style, consider including it in your repertoire.

Avoid: Fashion Faux Pas

If you would like to be taken seriously, you need to avoid the following fatal mistakes.

1. Short sleeves

2. Strong cologne

3. Too much hair product

4. Excessive jewellery

5. Wrinkled or unkempt clothes

6. Ill fitting garments

7. Scuffed or tatty shoes

8. Visible tattoos or piercings

9. Rubber sports watch

10. Bow tie or suspenders

11. Excessive facial hair

CONCERNS

With all the guidance provided and even some myths debunked, I know there are still some of you who have concerns over your appearance. So let's address this before we continue forward.

For those of you with minor or temporary imperfections, such as the occasional pimple or patch of dry skin, I understand that a spot in the middle of your forehead is not ideal, but it isn't a disaster either. Recruiters are human too and will recognise that this is a temporary imperfection and will not base a hiring decision upon it. Likewise if you have a perceived flaw, such as an unusual face shape, off white teeth or a slightly crooked nose, these are characteristics that make you unique and are highly unlikely to make any sort of impact to the strength of your candidacy. So please stop worrying about extremes and focus your attention on what really matters.

On the other hand, if you do have a real concern, such as rosacea, acne, birthmarks or severely stained teeth, it is unfortunate that such appearance concerns can be cause for discrimination, so it really is worthwhile looking into treatments that may be available to you. With the advances in technology, it would appear that nothing is beyond fixing these days, so there is usually a treatment that will work for you.

For scaring, there are non-evasive laser procedures that can drastically minimise their appearance and for acne, there is medication and lotions. For rosacea, dark circles or birthmarks, you will find medical strength concealers and for stained teeth, cosmetic dentistry or tooth whitening procedures. Whatever path you ultimately decide to pursue, it is important to proceed with safety and due consideration.

In Conclusion

While the advice and guidance given in this chapter may sound obvious, unnecessary and, even, unimportant, it has been my experience that many candidates fail to create an impression because they are either confused or uninformed about the standard of dress expected of them or because they neglect to pay enough attention to the details.

Following this guidance will not only multiply your chances of attracting the interviewers attention, but you will also stand out for having made an extra effort.

In the grand scheme of things, it does not matter how well you are dressed or how much effort you have gone through if the rest of your delivery is poor. So, continue reading and you will discover important steps that will make you truly memorable.

You can't depend on
your eyes when your
imagination is out of focus

– *Mark Twain*

CREATE THE
RIGHT
IMPRESSION

YOUR COMMUNICATION

Because effective communication skills are essential for interview success, it is important to be mindful of how your communication is received. This means that you must consider not only the words you use, but also how your tonality and body language complement or contradict those words.

Consider the following communication guidelines:

Word choice

Words are important because they communicate and convey your message succinctly. So, even at a low 7% accountability, your word choice can mean the difference between a powerful, captivating and influential exchange, and a weak, disempowering and ineffective one.

 ### Action words

Action words are positive, powerful and directive, and should be used abundantly. Action words include: Communicated, conveyed, directed, listened, persuaded, arranged, handled and improved.

Filler words

Filler words are useless and annoying verbal mannerisms such as "you know," "huh," "erm," "kind of," "ummm," and "uh". Besides sounding unprofessional, they also distract attention from the message. Filler words should be avoided at all costs.

Undermining words

Words and phrases such as 'I think,' 'I hope,' 'maybe,' 'sort of,' 'perhaps,' 'I guess,' all undermine your message and credibility by creating the impression that you don't trust your own knowledge or opinion. Eliminating these phrases will drastically improve the quality of any message.

Jargon, slang and cliches

Specialist terminology and informal expressions can confuse an outside audience. Avoid these where possible, and stick to simple, clear and coherent language.

Vocal quality

Tonality plays a key role in sending the correct messages. So, if your aim is to project confidence, enthusiasm and expertise, it is important to exercise control and awareness of your tonality throughout your interactions.

Pitch

Pitch refers to the degree of highness and lowness in your voice. A variation in your pitch creates meaning, adds clarity and makes what you are saying more interesting. For instance: A rise in your pitch suggests you are asking a question, which indicates doubt, uncertainty and hesitation. A fall in pitch indicates a statement, which suggests certainty and assurance.

Tempo

Tempo refers to the speed of your voice. If you speak too slowly, you risk losing the interest and attention of your audience. If you speak too fast, others may find you difficult to follow. The key is to maintain a pace, which is fast enough to maintain interest, yet slow enough to be clear.

Volume

Speaking in a loud volume suggests aggression, while a quiet volume indicates shyness and makes it difficult to be heard. The key to determining the appropriate volume is to keep your voice loud enough to be heard, but soft enough to be clear. Modulation of volume can also be introduced to keep your speech interesting and add extra emphasis.

Articulation

Articulation refers to vocal clarity. Regardless of our pitch, tempo, volume and accent, you need to make a conscious effort to enunciate clearly.

Communication Barriers

Barriers to effective communication may arise for a number of reasons. When these barriers do occur, you are forced to become even more effective in your ability to communicate. The strategies below will help overcome some of these more effectively.

Language

If you struggle with the native language of the airline, or have a very strong accent, speak slowly and clearly, ask for clarification and check for understanding, avoid idioms and jargon, use gestures and be specific, listen actively and be patient.

Cultural

Because every culture has its own set of values, beliefs and behaviours, the potential for confusion and misunderstanding is high. Even when we speak the same language, these differences can lead to challenges. To effectively connect with an individual from a culturally different background, it is important to be sensitive and respectful, avoid prejudice and stereotyping, and be aware of using questionable language and gestures.

Gender

Barriers in communication between genders exist primarily because men and women have different communication patterns. To overcome these barriers, it is important to appreciate, learn and understand the different strengths and styles that exist.

While men tend to be more direct and factual, women tend to be indirect and tactful. Men have a preference for reason and logic, are competitive and are interested in power, rank and status. Women are empathetic and feeling oriented. They value relationships and like to build rapport. Men communicate to exchange information and solve problems, while women communicate to share and a build connection.

Emotional

Emotional barriers within an interview situation manifest themselves through fear, shyness or restraint. When we feel distracted by these emotional states, our ability to communicate at an effective level is severely inhibited. We may wrongly interpret the actions and words of others, and may not effectively express our own opinion. We may even stop listening to the other person as our internal dialogue takes over.

To effectively deal with these barriers, it is important to treat the underlying cause of such emotions.

Let your body
DO THE TALKING

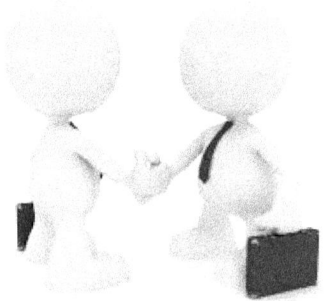

The way you carry yourself, the gestures you use and your facial expressions communicate all sorts of messages. If you appear to lack confidence, seem evasive, or exhibit negative body language it is only natural that the interviewer will want to dig further to find out why your body is contradicting your words. So it is worth learning to control certain aspects so that you can convey the message of a well-balanced, confident individual.

The reason why your body language is so important is that it supports and reinforces what you say. In essence you appear to be exactly what you say you are.

Gestures

We use open gestures when we are feeling confident and relaxed, and are being honest and sincere, therefore, keep your arms unfolded, your legs uncrossed and your palms open. Sitting or standing with your arms crossed will be interpreted as a defensive posture and will give the impression that you are uncomfortable, bored, or have something to hide. Likewise, standing in your hands in your pockets suggests unease.

Touching your nose during the interview is commonly interpreted as an indication of dishonesty, so even if it itches, it is best to grin and bear it. Observe caution if you experience the tendency to rub your neck as this too can be misinterpreted as boredom or unease.

Gesturing can be useful for adding emphasis to what you are saying and, if the movements you employ are subtle and controlled, it is perfectly okay to use gestures to express yourself and endorse your words. For best results, keep any movements below shoulder level, but above the waistline.

Posture

Posture is fundamental to appearing alert, confident and motivated, and yet it is shocking to see how many candidates forget this one simple rule. Take a look around the room next time you attend a group interview and you will see candidates slouching and generally looking bored and inattentive while they wait to be assessed.

I understand that the wait can be long and tiresome, however, it is important that you do not let this happen to you. This is the period when you are being watched very closely and letting your posture relax too much will demonstrate disrespect and give the impression that you lack interest.

To portray the image of a confident and motivated person, adopt an upright and attentive posture that is open, yet relaxed. Keep your chin parallel to the floor, shoulders back and spine straight.

If seated, lean slightly forward with your hands loosely in your lap, or on the table. Place both feet flat on the floor, or cross your ankles. And always be sure to direct your body and your feet towards the interviewer and not at the door, as this will give the impression that you feel uncomfortable and are ready to flee.

If standing, keep your arms loosely at your side or behind your back and plant your feet about 8-10 inches apart. If standing for long periods, place one foot slightly in front of the other to allow you to smoothly and unnoticeably shift weight between your feet.

Your carriage

The way you carry yourself is a powerful indicator of how you feel. To be perceived as confident and professional, walk briskly with an erect posture. Keep your shoulders back, your arms loosely at your side, and chin parallel to the floor.

Facial expressions

Your facial expressions convey a wide range of attitudes, feelings and emotions, and these can have a significant impact on your ability to connect with others. Because of this, it is important to be aware of the story your face is telling and work to convey an attentive, sincere and interested expression.

A positive expression can certainly include a smile, but doesn't necessarily imply its inclusion. In fact, maintaining a constant smile is not only uncomfortable, but it is also completely unnecessary. Instead, an open expression that includes a gentle and understated smile, soft eyes and slightly elevated eyebrows will result in a soft and pleasant expression.

Large smiles should be reserved for introductions and the occasional injection during conversation.

Handshake

Your handshake says a lot about you. A firm handshake conveys confidence, assertiveness and professionalism while a weak, limp handshake suggests shyness and insecurity. A strong, crushing handshake indicates aggression and dominance, and should be avoided.

To perform a professional and confident handshake, follow these simple guidelines:

Before connecting for the handshake establish eye contact, smile and lean slightly forward. As you extend your right hand, keep your hand straight and thumb pointing upwards. When your hands connect engage a firm, but not crushing, grip. Pump one to three times, for a duration of 1-3 seconds, and break away.

DEFINITELY HAVE IT

Good eye contact is one of the most important factors of body language. Shifty eyes, or complete avoidance of contact can suggest dishonesty, boredom, rudeness, insecurity or shyness.

If you find eye contact anxiety provoking and uncomfortable, direct your gaze at their eyebrows, forehead, or bridge of the nose. This is not a permanent solution by any means, but it will certainly ease you into the process.

In an attempt to forge eye contact, be aware not to stare as this can indicate aggression and make others feel uncomfortable. To avoid this extreme, lighten your gaze and keep it friendly. This can be achieved by allowing your eyes to go slightly out of focus.

If you have notes, you can temporarily break eye contact as you refer to these, and if there is a second recruitment officer present, this will give you opportunity to break eye contact as you periodically direct your focus back and forth between the two.

Aim to maintain eye contact for 80-90% of the time.

Caution:

SMOKERS

Due to the non-smoking environment on board an aircraft and the fact that you will not be able to step outside for a quickie mid-flight, many airlines now have a strict no smoking policy and will not hire smokers. So if you are partial to a cigarette or two, it is important that you refrain from 'sparking up' at any time before or during the interview, as the smell of smoke will linger on your clothing. Once the interview is over, you may of course have one, but be sure you are well away from the building.

To avoid your interview garments becoming infested by the smell of stale smoke, have your outfit cleaned thoroughly and then keep it zipped up in a suit bag away from your smoking environment. On the day of your interview, be sure to wash thoroughly before you handle it.

Although it is possible to try to conceal the smell of smoke, the effort required and the risks involved are far too great

and it simply isn't worth it. The best course of action on the day of the interview is to wear a nicotine patch.

If you find the thought of not smoking for the day too much to bear, temporarily switch over to e-cigarettes, but be sure to use it only within the privacy of the W.C. and never in public view.

So, what should you say if you are asked whether you smoke? Well, this will depend on you. You can of course say no, you could be tactful with the truth and simply state that you have recently given up or you can respond in the affirmative. Whichever answer you choose is your decision, but beware that being honest in this instance may be the quickest way for your resume to hit the rejection pile.

In fact, you will find that many airlines now have this as part of the employment contract, so it is worthwhile considering kicking the addiction in the long term.

I influence anybody who
is able to get through
the chaos of my first
impression.

- *Gary Vaynerchuck*

CREATE A
MEMORABLE
IMPRESSION

MEMORABLE IMPRESSION

When faced with hundreds, and possibly thousands, of other candidates, merely creating a good impression just isn't enough. You need to be memorable. The trouble is, very few people know how to truly differentiate themselves from the competition. Most candidates enter the interview in their own little bubble, thinking that they only need to dress well and sell their skills and experience. Unfortunately, this is only a small part of it.

Creating a memorable impression goes far beyond what you wear and how you carry yourself, and even beyond the skills and experience you posses. In fact, it is so rare that only 2% of candidates ever make it through to being hired.

The secret to creating a memorable impression will surprise you in its simplicity, and yet many candidates are unaware that such an advantage even exists, let alone know how to evoke it. They often enter the process only prepared for the hard sell, if they are prepared at all, and end up merely blending in with the rest of the crowd.

Recruiters see this same thing time and time again, so any candidate who is prepared to put in just that little bit of extra effort will naturally stand out, and it is these candidates who, ultimately, get hired.

So what is this mysterious phenomenon and how can you use it to your advantage?

OF THE CONNECTION

This technique is actually not mysterious at all. In fact, it is not even a secret. The technique involves creating a connection or, most commonly referred to as, establishing a rapport. Rapport is such a powerful tool, as it is the quickest way to achieve a sensation of familiarity and trust between you and the recruiter. It is so powerful, in fact, that it can even sway the hiring decision in your favour.

Why does this technique work so well? Have you ever met someone for the first time and yet you felt a strong connection, just as if you'd known him or her forever? This is rapport in action. If you can establish this level of rapport with the recruiter or undercover officers, you can be sure they will remember you favourably.

The quickest and easiest way to achieve a connection this strong is through the act of mirroring.

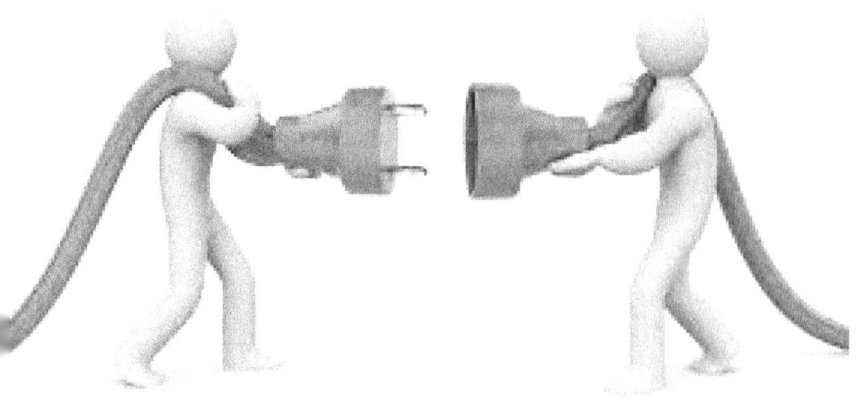

Mirroring is a process whereby you match your communication style, posture and mannerisms to those of another person. It is something you do naturally when you are deep in rapport with another person and is created by a deep feeling of unity. Using it consciously can evoke the sensation that the two of you are very much in sync just as readily as if it had occurred at a subconscious level, only you can be in control and use it to your own advantage.

As a note of caution, mirroring is something that must be done subtly to be effective. As such, it is important not to match every movement and not to react instantly to every change, else your motives will become obvious and the effectiveness of the technique will be lost.

For seamless results, take note of the following guidelines.

Body Language

As you are speaking with the recruiter, make a mental note of how they are sitting or standing, and what they are doing with their hands. Then, subtly mirror their position and gestures. If they are leaning forward, you might lean forward also. If they have their hands clasped on the table, you might do the same.

The best time to mirror a position is when you engage in dialogue. For example: The recruiter leans forward as he or she begins to ask you a question. As you engage in your follow up response, a change in position would appear natural and go completely unnoticed.

Be cautious not to mirror any closed signals, such as crossing your arms, as this will only accomplish a negative connection.

Communication Style

Mirroring a communication style can be done through using similar words or phrases, matching the sensory style, or mimicking the pitch, tempo and volume of their voice.

Words and Phrases

You can make a fantastic psychological impact simply by injecting the recruiter's own terminology and sequence of words into your answers. For example, if the interviewer points out that they are looking for and value a candidate who is 'team spirited', inject the same phrase into your answer. Simply stating that "I work well in a team", or "I am a team player", while implying the same values, will not create the same strong psychological impact as using the interviewers own words.

Pitch, Tempo and Volume

Matching your pitch, tempo and volume to the recruiters speaking style will make you appear in tune to what they are saying. This will speed up the rapport process and greatly improve your chances of creating a favourable impression. Keep pace with the interviewer and assess their basic conversational style. If they have a fast pace, assume the same characteristics. If they are analytical and introspective, slow down your responses to their speed.

Sensory Style

While we all use a mix of the sensory styles: Visual, kinaesthetic and auditory, we tend to have a dominant style that we gravitate towards. If, during the course of the interview, it becomes obvious that the recruiter has a preference towards a particular sensory style, you can adjust your style accordingly to establish a deeper connection.

Visual people use words that reflect their visual style, such as: 'I see what you mean', 'It looks to me like...', 'I imagine that...'

Auditory people use hearing words, such as: 'I hear what you are saying', 'We'll discuss this further', 'I hear you loud and clear'

Kinaesthetic people use action words, such as: 'It feels as if...', 'It slipped my mind', 'I have a solid grasp...'

Next time you are in a public place, observe how people who appear to be closely connected do these same things. You could even try this out for yourself next time you are out for lunch with a close friend or family member. In fact, because this technique can appear uncomfortable and awkward the first time you try it, practicing will, in time, make it almost natural and automatic, and you may even find that your relationships begin to blossom more than usual.

Leading is an influencing technique that can be used to judge the level of connection. For example: If you feel you have achieved rapport with the recruiter, you could change position or make a gesture to see If the recruiter follows your lead. If this does occur, you can be sure that you have established a strong connection. It the test reveals that the connection is not as strong as you thought, simply go back to mirroring to re-establish and strengthen the connection.

It is important to be perceptive to signs that the recruiter has become disconnected so that you can be proactive in re-establishing the connection.

Before attempting to reconnect, however, it is important to establish the accuracy of your perceptions because you may have simply misread the signal or it could be a by-product of a paranoid imagination. Similarly, the perceived signal may be a momentary motion that has no substance or it may be unrelated to you entirely.

To reliably determine the accuracy of your observation, you first need to scan for clusters of signals that are supportive of your perception. If you observe two or more congruent signals, this is a definite cluster. Next, you can test our connection by attempting to 'lead' (see above). If the recruiter doesn't follow, this is also a sure sign that a disconnection has taken place.

During the group stages, you will not have an opportunity to forge any kind of connection with the official recruiters, however, you will be up close and very personal with the undercover team and it is here that you will be focusing much of your attention during these early stages.

The trouble is, how do you know who is undercover and who is a candidate? Unfortunately ,you don't. As such, the only possible way to accomplish this task is to make this same effort with every candidate you meet. While this may seem like an arduous and inefficient task, your efforts will pay off many times over, as you will gain an advantage like no other. In the worst instance, you will come away with a few new friends.

During the latter stages of the final interview, you can refocus your efforts on the official recruiters. This is where the technique will really come into its own and you can use it to its full advantage.

WHO ALWAYS GETS THE JOB OFFER

As you can now see, there is always one type who gets the job offer, but it isn't the best looking one as myths and legend would have you believe. The simple truth is that recruiters hire those individuals that they personally like and feel a connection with.

The biggest mistake most candidates make is that they enter the interview focused only on themselves and miss any opportunity to make a connection. A candidate who makes an effort will not only come across as more genuine and sincere, they will also instantly differentiate themselves from the competition, so it is certainly worthwhile putting the extra effort into perfecting this technique.

OLD FRIENDS

Another trick, which can be used as an adjunct to the previous technique, is to think of the recruiter as a good friend. Now I am not suggesting you take this literally, or you risk appearing too informal and familiar, what I am suggesting is that you enter the interview in a natural and conversational frame of mind.

The point of this technique is to help you relax, but also to assist the interviewer in breaking the ice. Simply initiating some friendly dialogue as you first meet the recruiter will help you to create an aura of a warm and approachable person, but also one who is relaxed and confident. Such a personable approach can help the interviewer feel more comfortable in your presence and will certainly get the interview off to a great start.

Naturally you will want to use common sense here to avoid stepping over the invisible line, however, it is important to remember that most candidates will only be thinking about themselves. The interviewer will appreciate your effort to connect.

APPROACH

If there is just one more thing that can set one candidate apart from the rest, it is the expression of a sincere passion and enthusiasm for the job, airline and the opportunity. Sadly, many people believe that showing enthusiasm will be mistaken for desperation and, as such, suppress their enthusiasm in favour of the laid back and relaxed approach. The truth is, the laid back approach is often mistaken for indifference or disinterest, and this can severely hinder your chances of success.

Another misconception is that being enthusiastic means that you need to be loaded with energy and bouncing off the walls. This is bordering on excitement, rather than enthusiasm, and is not ideal either. As discussed previously, the idea is to match the tempo of the person you are speaking to, and injecting too much energy can make it difficult for others to relate and connect with you, not to mention exhausting. You can certainly be calm and still be enthusiastic.

So what exactly is enthusiasm and how can you use it appropriately?

Use it appropriately

There are several ways that you can display your enthusiasm. This could be through an eagerness and willingness to learn, your facial expression and smile, an expression of pride in your work, actively listening and asking questions, taking notes and even through your knowledge and research about the opportunity and the airline.

You can also be upfront about your enthusiasm by stating it directly. For instance, when asked "Why do you want to be cabin crew?", speak from the heart as you tell them your personal story and the steps you have been taking to achieve your dream. If you have a sincere passion for meeting people from different cultures, express it. If you have a genuine love for assisting in the comfort of others, use it. If you have been participating in volunteer work to enhance your skills for the position, tell them. This is truly where you will stand head over heels above the run-of-the-mill answers that they hear 95% of the time.

Don't underestimate the power

It sounds simple, and even, superfluous, when compared to tangible skills and experiences, however, do not underestimate the power of honest and sincere enthusiasm. It is contagious and will energise those around you. More importantly, recruiters will pick up on your positive energy and will sense that you will approach the job with vigour.

SURVIVAL 101

PART 3

Of this Session

Resolve common concerns

Manage your nerves

Bloopers, blunders & faux pas recovery

One important key to success is self-confidence. An important key to self-confidence is preparation.

- Arthur Ashe

RESOLVE COMMON
CONCERNS

COMMON CONCERNS

Challenge: Blushing

Go green
A purposeful green-pigmented concealer or foundation will minimise the impact of redness.

Seek medical advice
Blushing which is caused by a medical condition should be treated by a medical professional. Prescription medication may be prescribed.

Challenge: Cottonmouth

Cottonmouth is a natural and protective barrier, which is often caused by nerves. To minimise the effects, be sure to keep fully hydrated on the run up to the event. Fill up on water during breaks and periodically sip on water throughout the assessment.

You can stimulate saliva flow by adding a splash of lemon juice to your water bottle, sucking on sugar free candy or chewing sugarless gum. Gently biting your tongue can also activate the glands that stimulate saliva flow.

Avoid salty and sugary foods, alcohol (including alcohol based mouthwash), caffeinated beverages and tobacco products as these inhibit saliva flow and dry the mouth out further.

Challenge: Excessive sweating

Dress Colours
Black, navy and pure white will help disguise sweat marks, as will the camouflaging nature of patterns. Avoid: Light colours such as pale blue or grey.

Dress Fabrics
Wear breathable fabrics such as: 100% cotton, pima cotton, seersucker, linen, 100% wool, merino, and cashmere. Avoid: Corduroy, flannel, silk, polyester and polyester blends, nylon, and acetate

Dress Style
Wear loose fitting over and under garments for maximum airflow. Add layers, such as a suit jacket, waistcoat or cardigan, to disguise sweating.

Medicated Antiperspirant
Heavy duty, medicated antiperspirants can now be purchased for those who suffer from severe sweating. Products such as Drysol, Certain Dry® and Maxim can be purchased over the counter and are very effective at dealing with such challenges.

Keep fresh
During bathroom breaks, wash your hands with lukewarm water. Blot your hands dry with a tissue and finish off with a light mist of a clear antiperspirant. Avoid: Cold or hot water, air dryers and sticky antiperspirants.

Seek medical advice
Individuals with Hyperhidrosis may seek the advice of a medical professional or dermatologist. Both can advise and prescribe suitable treatments, such as: Prescription strength antiperspirants and Botox.

Challenge: Eye contact

Good eye contact is one of the most important factors of body language. Shifty eyes, or complete avoidance of contact can suggest dishonesty, rudeness or lack of confidence. If you find eye contact anxiety provoking and uncomfortable, the following techniques will certainly help.

Use a mirror
Practice your eye contact by using your own-mirrored image as a guinea pig. When you see yourself in the mirror every day, make a point of looking directly into your own eyes.

Fake it
Rather than look directly into the eyes, you can fake it by either directing your gaze at their eyebrows, forehead, or bridge of the nose. This is not a permanent solution by any means, but it will certainly ease you into the process.

Avoid staring
In an attempt to forge eye contact, you may begin to stare. This can indicate aggression and make others feel uncomfortable. To avoid this extreme, lighten your gaze to keep it friendly. This can be achieved by allowing your eyes to go slightly out of focus.

Use opportunities to break contact
If you have notes, you can temporarily break eye contact as you refer to these. Also, if there is a second recruitment officer present, this will give you another opportunity to break eye contact as you periodically direct your focus back and forth between the two.

Challenge: Going blank

Even with all the preparation in the world, our mind can betray us and draw a blank at the most inopportune moment. If this happens, take a deep breath, remain composed and employ some of the following techniques:

Refer to your resume
Your resume provides an immediate memory jog in these instances, so refer to it as and when necessary. You may also want to jot down some key words or phrases inside a professional looking notebook beforehand.

Wait a moment
You don't have to always answer questions immediately. It is perfectly permissible to pause and collect your thoughts before proceeding with a response. In fact, taking the time to think through your response can make you appear deliberate and thoughtful. Answering without regard for your answer can make you look impulsive.

Be honest
If you don't have relative experience in a particular area, or simply don't know the answer, you need to be honest and say so. At this point, you could offer an alternative and or related answer.

Stall
If you feel you can get away with it, reflect the question back to allow yourself a little more thinking time.

Stay composed
Some recruiters will purposely throw in some curve ball questions to see how you react to pressure and think on your feet. In these cases, the interviewer is probably more interested in observing your reaction than they are about the answer you provide. So, stay calm and do your best to answer in a confident manner. In the worst case, simply be honest and admit you don't know the answer.

Challenge: Involuntary facial motions

Unless there is a medical condition present, involuntary facial twitching and trembling are generally ensuing of overly stressed muscles, such as forced smiling. These distressing symptoms are especially pronounced during an interview when you feel compelled to smile, or are attempting to conceal your nerves. To gain relief from these symptoms, you simply need to control how and when you smile.

Maintaining a constant grin is not only unnecessary and uncomfortable, it will also look insincere. Gentle and understated smiles are more than appropriate for prolonged periods, and full-toothed smiles should be reserved for introductions and the occasional injection during conversation.

Next time you feel your facial muscles begin to tense, try relaxing your smile and see what a difference it makes.

Challenge: Vocal paralysis

Under severe pressure, your voice may become partially paralysed. The physical symptoms of this may include stuttering, a weak and shaky vocal tone, or an unusually high pitch. These symptoms can be managed by adopting the following techniques:

- Speak in shorter phrases
- Slow your pace
- Control your breathing by using steady in-out breaths
- Maintain an upright posture
- Ignore the symptoms until they naturally relieve themselves
- Seek the assistance of a vocal coach

Challenge: Fidgeting

Fidgeting, tapping and excessive gesturing with give the appearance of uncertainty, nervousness and unpreparedness. To effectively manage these movements, use the techniques outlined below.

Identify
If you are unsure of any habits you may have, ask a friend, partner or co-worker for their views. Alternatively, record yourself in a short mock interview and examine the footage. Mark down any ineffective mannerisms you can identify (playing with your pen, drumming your fingers, touching your face or hair, clearing your throat, or rubbing your nose) and then begin the process of consciously eliminating each of them.

Beware of props
Props can easily exaggerate any fidgeting, so if you have a pen, résumé or bag with you, avoid fiddling with them. Be equally mindful of jewellery, such as twirling earrings or a finger ring.

Mind your hands
If the movements you employ are subtle, it is perfectly okay to gesture your arms and hands to endorse your words. Subtle means, keeping the movements below shoulder height and above the waist. If you find your movements become excessive or distracting, simply intertwine your fingers and rest your hands on the table or clasped loosely in your lap.

Challenge: Perceived arrogance

Sometimes, a high level of confidence may be misconstrued as arrogance. If you feel you are sometimes wrongly labelled as arrogant, the following guidelines will help you maintain your confidence, while avoiding this assumption.

Be open
We all have weaknesses; to say otherwise will certainly make you appear arrogant. Be clear about what you do and don't know, and be prepared to listen and learn from others.

Be humble
Act with humility when you are recognised for a job well done. Acknowledge the effort of others by sharing and giving praise where appropriate, and be accountable when errors transpire.

Be approachable
To make yourself appear more approachable, use open and inviting body language, and adopt a warm, friendly expression. Inject some personality into your conversations, make good use of eye contact and remember to use people's names.

Be considerate
Genuinely acknowledge and compliment the hard work and efforts of others. Listen to and respect others opinions, and avoid interrupting when others are speaking.

Challenge: Being alienated

When there are a lot of different personalities in a group and the emotions are high, it can become difficult to get involved. This is especially true during a large group discussion. In these instances, you should employ some of the following strategies for getting your voice heard.

Raise your hand
As simple as it seems, raising your hand will demand the attention of the group and let them know that you have something to say.

Be assertive
If raising your hand reaps no results, you will have to be more assertive. Wait for a momentary pause in the conversation, and simple say, "excuse me" before proceeding. This may feel uncomfortable for some of you, but it is imperative that you contribute. If done calmly and respectfully, the assessors will be impressed by your effort.

Challenge: Being ridiculed

If your idea is ridiculed, resist the temptation to retaliate. Instead, remain cordial and respectful in your response. This graceful reaction will be duly noted and respected by the assessors.

Challenge: Handling disagreements

If you disagree with an approach being taken by the group or an idea, which has been brought forth, it is perfectly reasonable to say so as long as you are constructive and positive in doing so.

Consider the following statements:

Negative:
"That wouldn't work. I think we should..."

Constructive:
"I see your point, Mark, but there are a number of issues that may arise with that approach. How about we consider..."

The former example attacks and ridicules the idea, while the latter demonstrates a positive acknowledgement before a new idea is introduced.

In the instance that your new idea is rejected, remain polite and seek input from the group. If you are clearly outnumbered, gracefully accept the decision and move on.

Challenge: Feeling uncertain

You don't always have to give an opinion when you speak. Supporting what someone else has said, asking a legitimate question, or commenting on an emerging theme are equally good ways to make your presence known without appearing as if you like the sound of your own voice.

Points to Consider

In most cases, the outcome of each task or topic is largely irrelevant. Assessors are more concerned with how well you perform in a team environment, how you communicate your ideas and interact with others, and what role you typically assume.

Thus, no matter how you feel, you should approach every task with a can do attitude and every topic in a calm and conversational tone.

Find out what you like doing best and get someone to pay you for doing it

- *Katharine Whitehorn*

MANAGE YOUR
NERVES

YOUR NERVES

Nervous feelings before an interview are quite legitimate and most people can relate to feeling tense or fearful on the run up to such an event. In fact, a little interview anxiety can make you more alert and really enhance your performance, so you would never want to completely eliminate interview anxiety. However, when that anxiety becomes strong enough to negatively affect your clarity of thought and dialogue, some anxiety management techniques must be introduced.

AND PREVENTION

 ## Interview preparation

Anxiety can be the result of poor preparation. If you anticipate potential questions, prepare appropriate answers, research the airline and understand the requirements of the job, you will be better mentally prepared. If your mind is prepared, you will naturally feel calmer and more confident in yourself, and your ability to handle the interview.

 ## Remediation

Hypnotherapy, Cognitive Behavioural Therapy (CBT) and Neuro Linguistic Programming (NLP) sessions are very effective at dealing with deep-rooted anxiety issues.

 ## Medication

If you find your anxiety levels quite literally overwhelm you at interviews, you may be considering medication. While this is a method I don't personally advocate due to long-term side effects, there are over the counter supplements, such as Kalms, St John's Wort, and Bachs Rescue Remedy, which can really help take the edge off anxiety. Otherwise, your medical practitioner may prescribe stronger prescription medications such as Xanex or Beta Blockers.

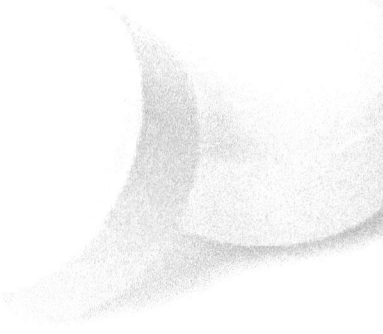

Manage your mindset

Limiting beliefs are erroneous assumptions you hold about your own capabilities. They lurk in your subconscious mind and lead to self-sabotaging behaviours, which prevent you from achieving your desired goals. These beliefs are mostly acquired subconsciously through outside influences and, once accepted and imprinted into your subconscious mind, will dictate how well you perform, interact and grow.

To move forward, these limiting beliefs must be identified and challenged, and then replaced with more empowering beliefs.

Step 1: Identify

Clearly it would be impossible to challenge or change a belief that you are unaware of, so the first step to transformation involves identification.

Some limiting beliefs are obvious and can be easily identified by their all or nothing words, such as 'always' 'never', 'can't' or 'impossible'. For instance:

- My confidence always lets me down
- There's too much competition. I can't possibly compete
- The interviews are impossible
- I never say the right thing
- I always fail

Some beliefs, however, are so deeply ingrained within your subconscious that you may not even be aware of their existence. To expose these, you can use a brainstorming session.

Brainstorming is a simple, yet powerful, technique that produces raw material from the subconscious mind. To begin, simply sit down with a pad and pen, and start writing down everything that comes to mind about the interview.

If you struggle for a place to begin, you could use the opening line "I want to pass the cabin crew interview but..." then proceed to fill in the page until you run out of buts.

Asking relevant questions may also help, for instance:

- What meanings could I have created based on my past disappointments?
- What pessimistic thoughts reoccur every time I think about the interview?
- What unnecessary assumptions do I make about the interview?
- How might my standards be affecting my ability to relax?
- Am I holding onto any stereotypical beliefs that are holding me back?

Step 2: Challenge

Now that you have identified your limiting beliefs, the next step is to challenge them. By challenging your old beliefs, you create doubt. This doubt is all you need to be able to slot a new empowering belief in its place. Strong beliefs are not always easy to destroy. These can, however, be weakened when they are challenged.

Challenge the beliefs directly

The first way to break down a limiting belief is to question its validity. Challenge yourself to find evidence against it, and build a case that proves the assumption wrong. You could ask yourself questions, such as: How do I know this? Is it impossible or just hard? Is there another way I could look at this? Could there be another truth here?

Question the source

Do you know where your assumptions came from in the first place? Did you choose these beliefs or are they by-products of someone else's belief systems? Sometimes, realising a belief is not yours is enough to destroy it.

Challenge their usefulness

During your life, you have picked up beliefs that have not served you or were only valid for a certain period, but you have held onto them ever since. Ask yourself: Does this belief still serve a useful purpose? Does it help me move closer to my goals? Does this belief help or hurt me? If this belief limits me, how can I quickly get rid of it?

Weigh the consequences

The avoidance of pain is a great motivator, so realising the negative consequences of your beliefs may provide the motivation you need to destroy it. Ask yourself: What has this belief cost me in the past? If I don't change this belief now, what will the consequences be in the future?

Step 3: Replace

In this final step, you will identify and install alternative empowering beliefs. To do this, you simply need to reinforce each new belief with sufficient evidence to support it. Ask yourself: What have I done in my past that could contribute as evidence? What activities and actions could I take now that would strengthen this belief?

Keep a journal and continue creating evidence towards it. The more ingrained you can make the belief, the more evidence it will begin to identify for itself, and the deeper rooted the belief will become.

This step isn't an overnight process. It does take time to imprint the belief deeply enough into your subconscious that it will stick long term and overpower the old limiting belief but, with repetition and reinforcement, positive changes will begin to happen in your life.

Use your imagination

Since your brain knows no difference between real or imagined experiences, it is possible to use mental rehearsal and visualisation techniques to manipulate your physiology and improve your interview performance.

Find a quiet space where you're unlikely to be disturbed for 10-15 minutes and use these basic guidelines:

Get into a comfortable position and allow your body to relax. Take a few deep breaths and, as you exhale, imagine all of the tension slowly leaving your body.

Now imagine it is the day of your interview and begin to visualise the entire day, scene by scene, in your subconscious. When running through the events in your mind, imagine feeling relaxed, yet energised as you converse effortlessly with other candidates and the recruiters. Observe how others warm to your friendly and confident nature. Imagine your composure as you intelligently answer the interviewer's questions.

Make each scene as vivid and real as you can. Bring it closer, make the colours richer, sense the atmosphere in the room, and introduce sounds and feelings. Really intensify the experience.

When you are pleased with the imagined performance, begin to introduce challenging scenarios for different characters you may encounter, questions you may be asked, and pressure you may be put under.

Using this rehearsal technique for just twenty minutes a day will train your brain to actually perform the new skills and behaviours.

Repetition is the key to success with this technique. The more you practice, the better you will get and the more confident you will feel.

Anchor your state

Anchoring is an NLP (Neuro Linguistic Programming) term, which describes a process whereby certain psychological states, positive or negative, become associated with and can be triggered by a certain stimulus.

Using certain techniques, it is possible to anchor positive states so that you can readily access them on demand, or you can break the association of undesirable states using collapsing techniques.

Create an anchor

Step 1: Identify
To begin the process of creating an anchor, you first need to identify the desirable state. For instance: confidence, calmness, and assertiveness.

Step 2: Locate a memory
Next you need to recall a particular time in your life when you have felt the desired state. The context is unimportant, but the experience must have been a powerful one.

Step 3: Get into state
With an experience in mind, mentally put yourself back into that experience. Use all your senses to make the experience as vivid and intense as you can. What did you see? What could you hear? Where there any smells present? How did you look? How did you feel? Now really focus in and intensify those feelings.

Step 4: Anchor the state
When the desired state has been captured and the feeling is about to hit its peak, it is time to anchor those feelings. This is done by firing off a unique combination of cues.

The cue combination can include one which is visual, one auditory, and one kinaesthetic. For example, pinching the skin above your knuckles, while visualising the colour blue, and saying the word 'YES' is a unique cue combination that would be appropriate.

Step 5: Repeat

To really condition the anchor, repeat this procedure at least five times. The more repetitions, the stronger the anchor will be.

Step 6: Test

Now that your anchor has been installed, you need to test its effectiveness. To do this, you simply need to fire off your unique cue combination that you set up in step 4.

For best results, break state for a few moments and think of something completely unrelated.

If the anchor has been a success, the desired state should be experienced within 10-15 seconds. If the feeling is not satisfactory, further reinforcement repetitions may be carried out, or the power of anchor stacking may be introduced.

Collapse and anchor

Step 1: Identify

Before you begin the process of collapsing an anchor, you first need to identify the problem state (e.g. panic, anger, anxiety) and decide an alternative desired state that you would like to create in its place (e.g. confidence, calmness, assertiveness).

Step 2 : Create

Next you begin the process of creating anchors (See above). First you will create an anchor for the desirable state you want to capture and then you need to repeat the process for the undesirable state you want to collapse.

In creating the se two anchors, you want to create the desirable anchor according to the steps outlined previously, however, the undesirable state should be created with less intensity in order to give the positive state more power.

This can be done effectively by simply visualising the negative state in less context, using fewer senses, and only using one kinaesthetic cue (be sure this cue is different to the one selected for the positive anchor)

Step 3: Repeat
To really condition the anchors, repeat the procedure at least five times. The more repetitions, the stronger the anchor will be.

Step 4: Test
Now that your anchors have been installed, you need to test their effectiveness. To do this, you simply need to fire off your unique cue combinations.

For best results, break state for a few moments and think of something completely unrelated.

If the anchor has been a success, the state should be experienced within 10-15 seconds. If the feeling is not satisfactory, further reinforcement repetitions may be carried out, or the power of anchor stacking may be introduced.

Step 5: Collapse
Finally, you can begin the process of collapsing your problem anchor.

To do this, you simply fire both anchors at the same time. As you do this, your physiology will feel somewhat confused as it tries to achieve both states simultaneously. If the positive anchor has been created strong enough, the negative anchor will begin to clear. At this stage, you can let the negative anchor release, while you continue to fire and hold onto the positive state.

Step 6: Test
To test the success of the collapse, break state for a few moments and try to re-fire the negative anchor. The result should be neutral. If the state persists the procedure may be repeated, using the power of stacking positive anchors.

Ask resourceful questions

When you ask questions of yourself, you prompt your mind to search your internal memory archive for reasons and/or evidence to support those questions. So, whether you ask an empowering question, such as: "How can I achieve this?' or "Why am I so lucky?" or a disempowering question, such as: "Why does this always happen to me?" or "Why can't I ever get this right?" your brain will work to bring forth answers.

Wouldn't you rather have your brain bring back answers that create happiness and success? Well, why don't you make yourself a commitment to only ask empowering questions of yourself from this point forward? It's simple to do, and will really enhance the quality of your life.

Replace:
"What's the point? I never pass anyway"
"I always get nervous in interviews"
"Why can't I be confident?"

With:
"What steps can I take that will increase my chances of success?"
"What can I do to manage my emotions?"
"How can I feel confident right now?"

Create Compelling Reasons

There may be challenging periods that arise during your interview, which cause you to question your motives. If you have compelling reasons for wanting the job, your conviction will give you the driving force you need to carry you through these challenging moments.

So, ask yourself:
Why do I really want this job?
How will this job change my life?
How will I feel when I am successful?
What would I enjoy about the job?

Affirm & Incant

Affirmations are short positive statements, which are repeated several times in order to impress on your subconscious mind. To perform an affirmation, you simply take your chosen statement, for example "I am confident and successful in everything I do", and repeat it several times in quick succession with all the conviction and passion you can muster.

An incantation is a supercharged affirmation, which also engages your physiology. This action of getting your body involved creates a much more powerful outcome.

Depending on how deeply ingrained your beliefs are, you may experience some strong resistance as your brain attempts to challenge the positive messages it is receiving. Thus, the effectiveness of both techniques relies on repetition, conviction and passion. The stronger your concentration, the deeper your faith and the more feeling you inject, the stronger the results will be and the faster changes will begin to occur.

Deep breathing

Deep breathing will steady your rapid heartbeat, strengthen your shallow breathing, provide your brain with vital oxygen and make you more alert. Be sure to expand your stomach as you breath in, and not your chest. This will allow a much deeper breath to be taken and will allow your lungs to fill with oxygen.

Change your focus

What you focus on has a direct impact on how you feel and what you experience. Therefore, anxiety is heightened the more you focus your energy on it. To gain some instant relief, you could try changing your focus. Instead of thinking about how you are feeling, how you look or what you are saying, re-focus your attention on outside sources. If you are engaged in dialogue you could listen more intently. Wherever you can redirect your focus will be much better than focusing on your internal dialogue.

Adjust your physiology

What you focus on has a direct impact on how you feel and what you experience. Therefore, anxiety is heightened the more you focus your energy on it. To gain some instant relief, you could try changing your focus. Instead of thinking about how you are feeling, how you look or what you are saying, re-focus your attention on outside sources. If you are engaged in dialogue you could listen more intently. Wherever you can redirect your focus will be much better than focusing on your internal dialogue.

It is never too late to be
what you might have been.

- *George Eliot*

BLOOPERS
BLUNDERS
AND FAUX PAS RECOVERY

TO THE BEST OF US

We've all experienced a blunder at some time or another, from the ill-fated slip of the tongue, to the embarrassing body blooper. You name it, it's happened to the best of us.

In everyday circumstances, bloopers, blunders and faux pas can be brushed off and, hopefully, forgotten. But what do you do and how can you recover if this happens during the all-important interview event? Do you laugh it off? Apologise? Pretend it never happened? Blame someone else? Make a sharp and speedy exit, or maybe a combination of the above?

Just in case the unexpected should happen to you on your big day, I have devised some stealth tactics and faux pas recovery tips. Hopefully you will never have to use them, but at least you'll have a strategy if you need one.

Three effective approaches

Depending on the severity of the blunder, there are three ideal approaches you can take: The first is to simply ignore it and move into a smooth recovery. The second is to hold yourself accountable and apologise, and the third is to simply laugh it off.

So let's take a look at each of these strategies further.

The smooth recovery

In many instances, you may choose to simply ignore it and move straight into a smooth recovery. This can be a great option if the blunder was mildly insignificant or barely noticeable. The risk with this strategy is that many will use it as a means to forge ahead and hopefully disguise their embarrassment. Unfortunately this urge to keep talking can make things worse if you are rattled or fixated on the blooper. Instead of making a smooth recovery, you may find yourself babbling.

After a blooper, it is natural to feel embarrassed, but it is important that you don't become fixated or concerned about the blunder or the recruiter. You'll stand a much better chance of recovery if you stop, take a breath, smile and continue on.

The artful apology

For moments that cannot just be ignored or brushed aside, there is the artful apology. Apologising for a blunder or faux pas is a great way to demonstrate a sense of respect and character. Rather than trying to hide or make excuses, drawing attention to the mistake and then apologising will demonstrate that you are honest and not afraid to take responsibility. This is an admirable quality and should not be underestimated.

Most people are willing to forgive, and you'll be amazed at how disarming a simple apology can be. Moreover, once a genuine apology has been made, the case is closed and everyone can move on from it.

It is important to keep your apology simple, yet sincere. A statement such as "I do apologise, my nerves got away from me there" or "I'm sorry, that came out wrong. May I rephrase that answer?" is all that is required. Once the apology has been made, shift the attention away and continue as if nothing happened. Don't give in to the urge to offer a lengthy apology, and don't bring the incident up again.

Be willing to laugh at yourself

When all else fails, having a laugh at your own expense may be the only way to disarm your audience and smooth over the faux pas. It will certainly lighten any awkwardness that has emerged in the atmosphere and most people appreciate someone who is willing to laugh at their own mistakes. If nothing else, it will show that are you aren't easily rattled and at least have a sense of humour. Not bad qualities I'm sure you'll agree.

It's how you handle it that counts

Whatever blunder you encounter, remember that everyone makes mistakes, and it is how you handle the mistake that will be observed and remembered. So whether it is the unexpected burst of flatulence, the skirt caught in the panties or a flubbed answer, if you are able to keep your cool and make a smooth recovery, the recruiter will appreciate your ability to remain composed in a challenging situation.

BOOST YOUR

CANDIDACY

PART 4

Of this Session

- Application guidance

- Resume guidance

- Produce polished photographs

- Power up your portfolio

If you change the way you look at things, the things you look at change

- Dr. Wayne Dyer

APPLICATION
GUIDANCE

It is true to say that job applications are primarily used to collect data for the purpose of evaluating skills, qualifications, employment history and motives, however, what most individuals don't realise is that there is an ulterior motive.

From the airline's perspective, the form serves a number of other important purposes, namely: To evaluate the applicant's literacy, ability to follow instructions, penmanship and communication skills. Recruiters will be looking or any excuse to thin the pack, so a careless applicant, or one who doesn't follow instructions, will quickly disqualify themselves, and the recruiter will not take the time to decipher what is written on it.

Unlike resume's, which are unique to each individual, the standardised format of an application form allows selectors to quickly peruse and compare each form, and it is easy to see which candidates have made an effort and those who haven't.

Consider the following examples.

I CURRENTLY WORK AS A FREELANCE HAIRDRESSER AND HAVE WORKED IN CLIENT FACING ROLES FOR MORE THAN 8 YEARS. I AM LOOKING FOR A CHANGE IN MY LIFE DIRECTION AND FEEL THAT A CAREER AS CABIN CREW WILL GIVE ME THIS.	*I curently work as freelance hairdresser & have worked in client facing roles fore more than 8 years. I am looking for a change in my life direction and feel that that a career as cabin crew will give me this.*

The first example is tidy and creates a positive impression of the candidate. Meanwhile, the second example is messy, full of typos and barely legible. It is clear that the candidate jumped straight in without planning. Hardly a positive first impression.

To ensure this doesn't happen to your application form, take note of the following guidelines.

Important

GUIDELINES

Before you begin

- Read through the form to familiarise yourself with the questions and any specific instructions
- Gather materials: Black pens, a pencil and eraser
- Gather the necessary information:
  - Personal details: Passport, contact information, vital statistics
  - Education and training information: Qualifications, dates, results
  - Employment History: Names, addresses, key dates
- Plan what you want to write in each section, taking note of the space available

Completing the form

- Set aside sufficient time and minimise distractions
- Re-read the instructions as you work on each section
- Write clearly and neatly: Block capitals are tidy and easy to read
- Keep your text within the space provided (Practice on a blank sheet of paper if you are unsure of the space available)
- Answer every question and use 'Not Applicable' or 'N/A' where questions are not relevant to you
- Keep the tone positive and be mindful not to volunteer negative information
- Be concise and avoid continuations on separate sheets of paper. If unavoidable, remember to clearly state your name and detail which part of the application form it is linked to

Finishing off

- If time permits, walk away for a few hours and return with a fresh pair of eyes
- Finish off with a quick proofread and make any necessary adjustments if there are typos, grammatical errors and inaccuracies
- If time permits, make a copy of the final form for future reference

Mailing off the form

- Select an envelope that is large enough not to require any folding of the form
- Address the envelope correctly and apply the correct postage
- Send it off before the closing date

THE TRUTH

If you are thinking about padding out your application form in order to increase your chances of being hired, you wouldn't be the first. Many candidates are tempted to stretch the truth either to gain a favourable advantage or as a means to cover undesirable facts.

Airlines are savvy to this idea and often verify the details you include within it. So, beware that exaggerations and untruths can come back to haunt you if you are quizzed about them at the interview, or later in employment. If you are caught, any future you may have had with the airline will be devastated.

What are the chances of your information being verified? 100%. This is an industry that places high importance on security, and an airline is not going to take any risks with providing airside passes to just anyone. Your references will be contacted and your background checked, so be safe and don't take any unnecessary risks. There are many things you can do to boost your candidacy and minimise imperfections, and it just isn't worth the risk.

A FRAGMENTED WORK HISTORY

A fragmented work history will give the impression of a job hopper and will raise serious doubts about your commitment. Whether the assumption is true or not, it surely doesn't present a favourable impression,

Whatever the reason, whether you have held temporary agency contracts, have been struggling to find something that you can feel committed to, or have simply been trying to gain a more rounded skill-set, it is important to draw attention away from it so that you can avoid any negative and rash assumptions being made.

Here are some options:

Eliminate

Where a position holds little or no relevance, was held only briefly, is dated, or was only held part time, you may be able to safely exclude it from your application. Beware that you should only do this if doing so will not create damaging gaps.

Spring into summer

Instead of listing specific dates for summer jobs, you can simply state Summer 20xx to Spring 20xx.

Consecutive combining

Where several similar consecutive jobs appear or were provided by the same agency, you can combine them into one chunk, for example:

2004–2006 Receptionist
Aztec Hotel & Spa, Bloomfields Leisure, Trina's Hair & Beauty Salon

2001–2003 Customer service manager
Multi-national business agency

Fill gaps in employment

If you have gaps in your employment history, you may be asked to elaborate on these. Whatever your reasons: whether it was for maternity leave, study or a travel break, you need to observe caution about revealing too much about your personal circumstances. Revealing that you had taken maternity leave will highlight your parental status and could be used as a tool to discriminate against you.

If you were doing anything during the gaps, paid or unpaid, inserting them in place of the gap will add much needed bulk and minimise the appearance of the gaps.

For example:

Summer 2004–Spring 2005   Travelled around Europe
July 2001–November 2001   Study break

TO BEING

When it comes to lying, there is one exception to the rule and that is if you have a termination on your record. The recruiters will not care if the termination was unjust, unfair or has a good explanation, a termination is a big red flag and will mark the end of your interview so you need to do everything you can to avoid disclosing it.

In the first instance, you may choose to omit the information. Omitting details is not the same as telling an outright lie or making a false statement. When asked for reference details, simply choose another referee.

If you have just been fired from your most recent employment, they will not know unless you tell them. So you could mark your employment to present and leave it at that. If asked if they can call your employer for a reference, it would not raise any eyebrows if you respectfully decline due to your ongoing employment.

The third option is to take proactive measures to have the termination designation changed. If the termination occurred some time ago, it is more likely that the employer will be open to changing the designation if you accept responsibility and demonstrate a sincere regret for the situation. Simply advise them that the termination is damaging your chances of gaining employment and you would like the designation changed to something neutral, such as laid off or resigned.

If you would feel uncomfortable or unethical to omit such a detail and would prefer to take accountability for what happened, be sure to downplay the termination on your application form by simply stating 'will explain at interview'. You will have some damage control to contend with, so remember to accept the mistake, don't blame others and don't make any excuses. Stick to the facts, point out what went wrong and what you have learned from the experience.

Whichever route you take, there is a risk. Either you not be hired by admitting to the termination or you may not be hired because you did not disclose it and were caught out. The decision has to be yours.

DISCRIMINATION

Unfortunately, age discrimination does occur within the airline industry, so you need to take proactive measures to you protect yourself if you are a mature candidate. Lengthy employment is often a clear indication of your age, as are graduation dates. In this instance, you may consider omitting dates and providing only a partial employment history. While this may only provide a temporary level of protection, at least you can buy yourself some time to demonstrate your suitability for the position before it comes to light.

YOUR SUITABILITY

The most important aspect of your application form is that you must communicate your suitability for the position clearly by highlighting the skills and experience that are relevant and transferable. Using a selection of key words that are often used to describe the cabin crew position will achieve this.

For example, a salon receptionist may include the following:

- Delivered the highest level of customer service
- Ensured customer comfort
- Provided a friendly and professional service
- Assisted with enquiries and resolved complaints

These short action statements identify customer service experience and the ability to handle specific responsibilities that are required of cabin crew. It would be clear to any airline that this candidate has the necessary experience and is adequately qualified for the position.

When describing your duties, three to five action phrases have a better impact than complete sentences or generic job descriptions. Consider the

ACTION PHRASES

following examples:

Complete sentence
'As a call centre officer, I answer customer queries and complaints over the telephone'

Action statement
'Addressed customer queries and resolved complaints'

The former example has a passive tone and is unnecessarily wordy, whereas the latter example uses an active and punchy tone. Such statements will grab the attention of the reader much more readily than lengthy paragraphs.

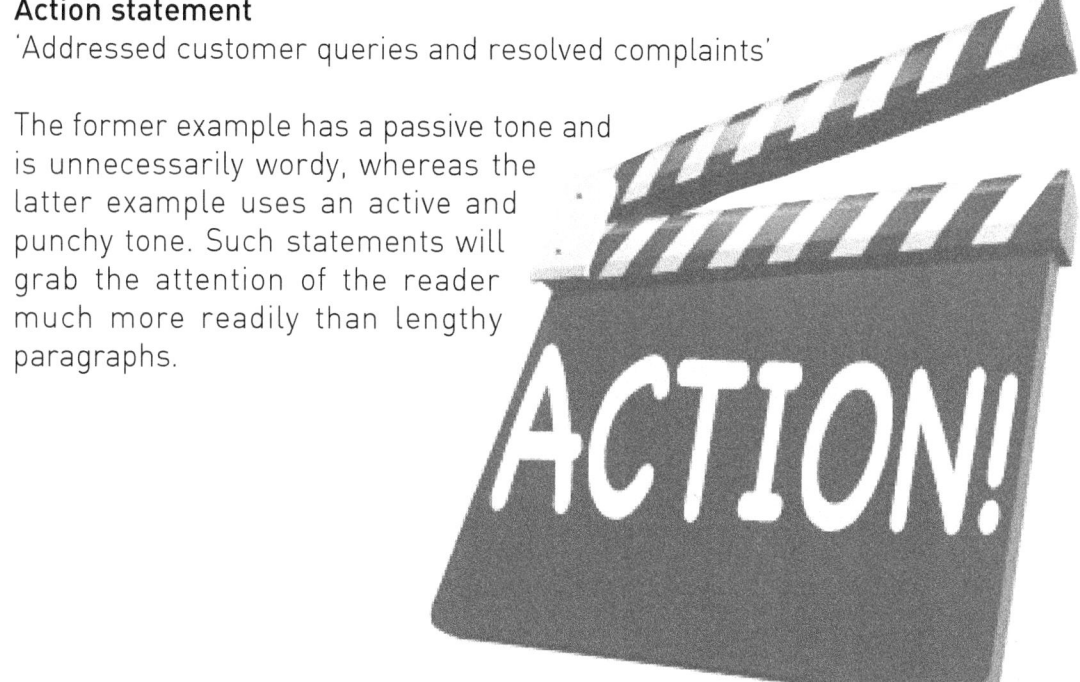

YOUR LEISURE INTERESTS

Recreational interests create depth and humanises your character. A targeted list, which focuses on relevant skills, will form an immediate and positive impression. Such interests also serve as excellent sources of additional skills and experiences, which can be advantageous if you lack relevant experience in a work environment.

Generalised list statements such as: 'reading, watching television, sport and socialising' should be avoided, as should unprofessional statements such as: 'I enjoy spending time with my mates, hitting the town and going out on the razz".

Take a look at the following example:

"I have been keen on netball for as long as I can remember and am an active member of my local netball club where I have been captain of the team for 3 years. I have an active interest in nature, and regularly get involved with and manage conservation assignments. To relax, I attend yoga and meditation classes, which help to keep me focused and relieve any build-up of stress.'

This statement gives an immediate impression of someone who is balanced and committed. Their interests highlight several admirable qualities such as team spirit and leadership, and it also details their methods of stress management. A recruitment office would form a positive impression of the candidate based on a statement such as this.

Be mindful about over-indulging in your leisure interests, as the recruiter may get the impression that your hobbies will take priority over your work.

OF A PERSONAL STATEMENT

At the end of most application forms, you will be presented with some form of additional information box. This box may simply state 'Additional Information', or it could be more specific, such as: Please state your reason for applying and why you feel you are suited to the position of cabin crew?

Essentially, this is an opportunity to sell yourself and should never remain blank. Use it to provide a power statement that summarises your experience, highlights your key skills, and shares your motives all within a few short paragraphs.

Consider the following example:

'As you will note, I have eight years experience within the retail industry. Within which, I have built extensive customer relations, team working and supervisory experience, which has also greatly enhanced my communication and interpersonal skills.

With these skills and experiences, combined with my passion for the airline industry, my motivation to succeed, strong attention to detail, and unparalleled work ethic, I am confident that I will make a positive contribution to the airline and excel as a member of the Fly High cabin crew team.

The above example is concise. It focuses on what the candidate can offer the airline, rather than what the airline can offer the candidate, and it showcases skills and experiences that are an asset for a cabin crew position.

Highlight career progression

If you have remained with an employer for several years, but have progressed through the ranks, you can make your progression more obvious by listing each position as you would a new job.

List your awards

Outstanding excellence will show commitment and talent, so if you have achieved any awards through your activities, be sure to list them. Make sure the achievements are recent though, as outdated awards may give the impression that you haven't achieved anything since.

Get permission from referees

Always get permission from the person(s) you state as your referee(s) and give them a copy of your application form or resume to help them write a relevant reference that highlights your most important points.

Fly High Airlines

Application for Cabin Crew Employment

All information supplied will be treated as confidential.
Subject to meeting the eligibility criteria, you will be invited to attend our next selection day.
Correct information will be a condition of employment.

Full Name (Mr / Mrs / Ms)   JANE DOE   Date Available   29/01/11

Present Address	Permanent Address (If different)
22 ANY STREET ANY TOWN ANY WHERE	N/A

Post Code	AN2 6DG	Country	U.K	Post Code	N/A	Country	N/A

Please give telephone numbers in the format: Country Code + City/Mobile Code + Phone Number

Telephone (Residence)	44 1179 637264	Telephone (Residence)	N/A
Telephone (Mobile)	44 798 837472	Telephone (Mobile)	N/A
Email	JANE.DOE@ANYMAIL.COM		

Personal Information

Passport Number:	2048374638	Expiry Date:	09/2021
Date of Birth:	11/09/1979	Gender:	FEMALE
Marital Status:	SINGLE	Nationality:	BRITISH

Height (cm)	154	Weight (kg)	49

Do you have tattoos or body piercings?	NO	If yes, please specify	N/A

How would you rate your ability to swim?   AVERAGE ABILITY UNAIDED

Education

Please continue on a separate sheet if necessary

From	To	Name & Address of School/College	Subject(s)	Results
09/99	07/01	ANY COLLEGE - ANY WHERE - AN8 7KD	HAIRDRESSING	NVQ 3 - DISTINCTION
09/98	07/99	ANY COLLEGE - ANY WHERE - AN8 7KD	HAIRDRESSING	NVQ 2 - MERIT
09/97	07/98	ANY COLLEGE - ANY WHERE - AN8 7KD	HAIRDRESSING	NVQ 1 - DISTINCTION
09/91	07/96	ANY SCHOOL - ANY WHERE - AN8 375	ENGLISH / GEOGRAPHY FRENCH / ART / CDT MATHS / SCIENCE / MATHS	8 GCSE'S GRADE A-C

Present/Last Employer

Employer:	SELF EMPLOYED	From:	01/02/03	To:	PRESENT
Position:	HAIRDRESSER	Salary:	15,000 PA	
Address:	N/A	Notice Required:	NONE	
		Reason for Leaving:	TO PURSUE A CAREER AS CABIN CREW	

Responsibilities:
MANAGE AND MAINTAIN A CUSTOMER BASE OF OVER 100 CLIENTS
CONSULT AND ADVISE CUSTOMERS
ENSURE CUSTOMER SATISFACTION
PROVIDE A FRIENDLY AND PROFESSIONAL SERVICE
MAINTAIN UP TO DATE RECORDS AND ACCOUNTS

Previous Employment   Please continue on a separate sheet if necessary

Employer: TRINA'S HAIR SALON
Address: 159 ANY CITY CENTRE ANY TOWN - AN9 6DJ
Position SENIOR HAIR STYLIST
Reason for Leaving: TO PURSUE FREELANCE OPPORTUNITY

From: 16/02/00   To: 01/02/03
Responsibilities: SUPERVISED AND TRAINED A TEAM OF FOUR JUNIOR-LEVEL STYLISTS - HIRED WORK EXPERIENCE STUDENTS - CONSULTED AND ADVISED CUSTOMERS - ENSURED CUSTOMER COMFORT AND SATISFACTION - PROVIDED A FRIENDLY AND PROFESSIONAL SERVICE

Employer: TRINA'S HAIR SALON
Address: 159 ANY CITY CENTRE ANY TOWN - AN9 6DJ
Position JUNIOR HAIR STYLIST
Reason for Leaving: TO PURSUE PROMOTION OPPORTUNITY

From: 05/04/98   To: 16/08/00
Responsibilities: CONSULTED AND ADVISED CUSTOMERS - ENSURED CUSTOMER COMFORT AND SATISFACTION - PROVIDED A FRIENDLY AND PROFESSIONAL SERVICE

Employer: MACEY'S HAIR SALON
Address: 378 ANY CITY CENTRE ANY TOWN - AN5 6SJ
Position RECEPTIONIST
Reason for Leaving: TO PURSUE PROMOTION OPPORTUNITY

From: 24/07/97   To: 05/04/98
Responsibilities: DELIVERED THE HIGHEST LEVEL OF CUSTOMER SERVICE - ENSURED CUSTOMER COMFORT - PROVIDED A FRIENDLY AND PROFESSIONAL SERVICE - ASSISTED WITH ENQUIRIES AND RESOLVED COMPLAINTS

Please explain any gaps in unemployment

UPON LEAVING SCHOOL IN 1996, I SPENT A YEAR TRAVELLING BEFORE MOVING INTO EMPLOYMENT

Please list any voluntary work

FOR THE LAST THREE YEARS, I HAVE VOLUNTEERED AT THE SAMARITANS HOMELESS SHELTER DURING THE CHRISTMAS PERIOD, WHERE I HELP COOK AND SERVE BEVERAGES

Additional Training
Give details of any first aid and/or nursing qualifications

BRITISH RED CROSS - BASIC FIRST AID TRAINING - 09/2006

Give details of languages spoken and abilities

ENGLISH - NATIVE LANGUAGE
FRENCH - READ, WRITE AND SPEAK FLUENTLY
SPANISH - BASIC CONVERSATIONAL ABILITY

Give details of any other training

I HAVE ATTENDED, AND PASSED, SHORT COURSES IN LEADERSHIP AND COMMUNICATION

Hobbies/Outside Interests

I HAVE BEEN KEEN ON NETBALL FOR AS LONG AS I CAN REMEMBER AND AM AN ACTIVE MEMBER OF MY LOCAL NETBALL CLUB WHERE I HAVE BEEN CAPTAIN OF THE TEAM FOR 3 YEARS. I HAVE AN ACTIVE INTEREST IN NATURE, AND REGULARLY GET INVOLVED WITH AND MANAGE CONSERVATION ASSIGNMENTS. TO RELAX, I ATTEND YOGA AND MEDITATION CLASSES, WHICH HELP TO KEEP ME FOCUSED AND RELIEVE ANY BUILD-UP OF STRESS

Use the following space to provide any further information that you feel will benefit your application

AS YOU WILL NOTE, I HAVE EIGHT YEARS EXPERIENCE WITHIN THE RETAIL INDUSTRY. WITHIN WHICH, I HAVE BUILT EXTENSIVE CUSTOMER RELATIONS, TEAM WORKING AND SUPERVISORY EXPERIENCE, WHICH HAS ALSO GREATLY ENHANCED MY COMMUNICATION AND INTERPERSONAL SKILLS.

WITH THESE SKILLS AND EXPERIENCES, COMBINED WITH MY PASSION FOR THE AIRLINE INDUSTRY, MY MOTIVATION TO SUCCEED, STRONG ATTENTION TO DETAIL, AND UNPARALLELED WORK ETHIC, I AM CONFIDENT THAT I WILL MAKE A POSITIVE CONTRIBUTION TO THE AIRLINE AND EXCEL AS A MEMBER OF THE FLY HIGH CABIN CREW TEAM.

Declaration
Have you ever been convicted of a criminal offence which, at the date of application, is not a spent conviction as defined in the Rehabilitation of Offenders Act 1974?   Yes/No
If yes, then such convictions must be disclosed below.

N/A

Have you ever been refused entry, or deported from a foreign country?   Yes/No
If yes, please provide further details.

N/A

The details provided on this application are correct to my knowledge and belief. I understand that my application may be rejected or that I may be dismissed for withholding relevant information or giving false information. I am aware that my employment with Fly High Airlines will be subject to satisfactory references, medical form and criminal record checks.

Signature   Date   05/01/2011

Don't tell me the sky's
the limit when there are
footprints on the moon

- Paul Brandt

RESUME

GUIDANCE

THE DIRECTION OF THE INTERVIEW

Because the recruiters will have no information about you beyond this document, it will be a major influence in the nature and direction of the interview. This allows an element of predictability and makes it a very powerful document indeed.

With such a valuable tool at your disposal, it is important that it represents the best you have to offer. If your resume is strong, it will focus the recruiter's questioning on information that presents your image strongly. The following guidelines will help you achieve this.

Colour

Use colour sparingly. Black text, with a consistent injection of colour for the headings will make your resume more pleasing to the human eye. Colour paper should be avoided as scanning or photocopying will be problematic.

Length

For this type of position, one or two pages is ideal. However, don't be constrained by this advice if doing so will mean that you have to squeeze your data in and use a tiny 8 point font, If you do find your resume going beyond this quota, be sure that it isn't being filled with unnecessary, unfocused or excessive detail.

Single or double sided?

Double sided prints are harder to photocopy and risk show through. Stick to single sided prints for a cleaner look.

Staples

Never staple your sheets together. Staples are inconvenient for the employer if they need to photocopy or scan your resume, plus the reviewer may want to view the pages side by side. A traditional paper clip is acceptable.

Identification

Be sure all of the pages include your name and page numbers so they can be easily reconnected should they become separated.

COULD BE DECIDING YOUR FATE

To facilitate more efficient processing of resumes, some larger airlines use a computerised tracking system. This system uses OCR (Optical Character Recognition) technology, whereby incoming resumes are scanned as a graphic image, converted back into text, read and added to the database.

With this in mind, it is important to write and format your resume in such a way that it can be successfully processed by these sophisticated systems. In this instance, the following guidelines apply:

The system scans your resume for keywords that indicate your skills, qualifications and experience. Following the scan, a score will be awarded based on the number of 'hits'. From this score, the system will either generate a letter of invitation, or a letter of rejection.

To ensure a high score, and an invitation letter, it is essential that you inject as many keywords as possible throughout your resume. The following highlighted keywords are the most widely scanned for:

- Good communication and interpersonal skills
- A confident and friendly personality
- Extensive customer service experience
- Confidence in dealing with a range of people
- The ability to work effectively in a team
- Ability to handle difficult customers firmly and politely
- Ability to stay calm, composed and focused under pressure
- The ability to be tactful and diplomatic, but also assertive when necessary

Action

VERBS

....

Action verbs express action. They are positive, powerful and directive, and should be used abundantly throughout your résumé.

Notice how using direct action verbs make the sentence powerful:

"As a hairdresser, I consulted with clients and provided advice"

The following page contains an extensive list of action verbs. Use them abundently throughout your resume and application form.
There are three basic resume formats:

CPSIA information can be obtained
at www.ICGtesting.com
Printed in the USA
BVHW011722251119
564774BV00007B/129/P